DOING IT FOR OURSELVES

DOING IT FOR OURSELVES

Success Stories of African-American Women in Business

Donna Ballard

BERKLEY BOOKS, NEW YORK

This book is an original publication of The Berkley Publishing Group.

DOING IT FOR OURSELVES

A Berkley Book / published by arrangement with
the author

PRINTING HISTORY
Berkley trade paperback edition / February 1997

The Putnam Berkley World Wide Web site address is
http://www.berkley.com/berkley

ISBN: 0-425-15613-3

BERKLEY®
Berkley Books are published by The Berkley Publishing Group,
200 Madison Avenue, New York, New York 10016.
BERKLEY and the ''B'' design
are trademarks belonging to Berkley Publishing Corporation.

PRINTED IN THE UNITED STATES OF AMERICA

10 9 8 7 6 5 4 3 2 1

Dedicated to
my mother, Larcia
for all your years of sacrifice

Philip Akers
for immeasurable support

Aunt Patricia Russell-McCloud
for teaching me courage

the memory of
Aunt Odessa Chambliss

and my children
for the years to come

Contents

Who's Who in
Doing It for Ourselves

Teri Agins	Senior Special Writer, *The Wall Street Journal*
Judith F. Aidoo	President and CEO, The Aidoo Group
Toni Banks	Account Executive, McGraw-Hill Companies
Cristal Baron	Public Finance, Merrill Lynch
Angela Brock-Kyle	Associate Director, Teacher's Insurance Annuity Association/ College Retirement Equity Funds
Lisa Caesar	Executive Director of Debt Sales, Peregrine
Bithiah Carter	Salesperson, W. R. Lazard
Teresa Clarke	Professor, University of Witwatersrand Graduate Business School, South Africa
Lisa Cowan	Consulting Analyst, Deloitte & Touche
Karen Gibbs	Anchor, CNBC's *The Money Wheel*
Carol Green	President, Laracris Corporation
Shahri Griffin	International Bonds Salesperson, BZW Securities, Inc.

Gail Gross Vice President in Training and Development, The Bank of New York

Carla Harris Vice President, Morgan Stanley

Wanda Hill Vice President in Marketing, The Bank of New York

Margot Lee President and CEO, Millennium Consulting

Brenda Neal Financial Consultant, Smith Barney

Lydia Payne Director of Advertising, Dean Witter

Benita Pierce President and CEO, B. Pierce & Co.

Sandra Stevens Manager of Current Programming, Fox Broadcasting Company

Jacquette M. Timmons President and CEO, Sterling Investment Management, Inc.

Gloria Turner Vice President, J. P. Morgan

Grace Vandecruze Associate, Corporate Finance, Merrill Lynch

Gay Young Literary Agent, Gay Young Literary Agency

I am tired of sailing my little boat
far inside the harbor bar
I want to go out where the big ships float
Out on the deep, where the great ones are

And if my frail craft prove too slight
For those waves that sweep the billows ore
I'd rather go down in the stirring fight than
drowse to death by the sheltered shore.

Anonymous

Acknowledgments

To so many, I am deeply grateful for their support on this effort. These accounts could not have been accomplished without the help of a few generous and concerned individuals who saw the need for this project. Although I cannot list every person who has made this project a reality, I would be remiss if I did not mention those who really invested their time and confidence in me and my ability to write. First, I would like to thank God for giving me the direction and revelation to write. God gave me the vision, internal peace, and patience to chronicle these much needed accounts for future generations. And to Him I am ever thankful. Next, I'd like to say thank you to my family (Mom, Dad, Toni, Lonnie, Art, Allycin and Shirley). To Philip Akers and Margot Lee, two of my good friends, thanks for giving me the biggest vote of confidence. Dawn Davis, thank you for putting me in touch with the right people and telling me to remain positive. Matthew Jordan Smith, thanks for helping in the initial stages of this project. Unfortunately, pictures were not used to illustrate this book but I still believe that you are the world's best photographer. Bill Thierfelder, thanks for assisting me in developing my ideas for this book. During the writing process, you became more than a suggestion box but a parallel spirit who knew with great depth what it was I wanted to do. Many, many thanks to Seth Washinsky, Steve Brighton, Leona Willis—thanks for keeping me going. Leslie Hill, a lifelong friend, thanks for providing me with the solitude to work during the final writing of this work. Alex Summers, Ericka Hall, Judy Sigh, Shaun Rowan, Carlyle Peake, Robert Hagans, Gregory Lacy, Larry Kantrowitz and Veronica Matarazzo, John Delaurentis, Brian Blakey, Alicia Holmes, Nan Saville, Ron Abad, Ericka Eaton, Leslie Shields, Rosena McNear, Sunni Aloci-Squire, Reginald Middleton, Jay Taylor, Willa and Frank Franklin, Rose Anderson, Robin Dunlop, Robin McCain, Jennifer Dargen, James Bryant, Baunita Greer, Edward Johnson, Zachery Jones, Walter Lancaster, Dauna Williams, Rev. Raphael Warnock, Robert Farmer, Shaka Rasheed, Peter Ongeri, Noel Edghill, Tracey Briscoe, Patricia Lester, Matthew Scott, Thais Rutledge, Thomas Powell, Nancy Gibson, Derek Penn, Michael Smart, Jacqueline Fields, Angela Durham, Rosanna Durruthy, my colleagues at New York University, the Wall Street Network for Women of Color. I could continue on *ad infinitum*, but then you would never get to read about many of the exciting and talented women that I have had the pleasure of meeting over the course of a year. Let me complete my list of thanks by saying thank you, Karen Thomas, my editor. Your time and patience has been a godsend. Thanks to all the women who permitted me a few moments of their time to talk about their professional lives. And thanks to those who agreed to participate but unfortunately could not be included.

Foreword

TWENTY-FIVE YEARS AGO IT WAS NEARLY IMPOSSIBLE to find as many women of color in positions of power and influence in the corporate world as you see today—nearly 3 million strong. Over the past two decades African-American women have redefined the expectations of what can be done in business in spite of racial and gender barriers. Equipped with an arsenal of degrees, distinctions, and professional designations, African-American businesswomen are positioned to enter the twenty-first century with more education, experiences, and opportunities than at any other time in our history. A March 1994 article in *The Wall Street Journal* cited black women as one of the fastest growing groups in the professional labor force between 1982 and 1992. While such phenomenal growth merits recognition, there are many challenges that we must face with the gains of crossing into uncharted territory. In addition to the continuing challenge to overcome the obstacles that have kept many of us from rising to our full potential in the greater society, a new challenge is emerging with our remarkable growth. And that challenge is to become more of a resource to one another. We have had a strong history in helping one another in this respect—in most instances to fight injustices still in existence. But in the business world, an environment in which we have only just started to have a notable presence, the rules of the game are much different and rarely spelled out. I have decided to direct my attention to creating a resource for other women in business careers. My hope is that future women can benefit from knowing many of the people I wish I had known before leaving Howard University in 1993 to enter corporate America. Although most of these interviews are with women who are from Wall Street firms or have left to start their own investment firms, several interviews are with women who work in industries such as publishing, fashion, and entertainment. Collectively their words weave together an informative discussion not only about how African-American women are making it in the business world, but also why we are achieving success. This book will show how these women have handled many of the issues that run parallel to being a successful person—transcending color and gender.

Profiles of this number and of this nature took many months of contemplation and even longer actually to write. The inspiration grew from knowing that these much needed interviews would someday find their way into the hands of you, the reader. During the toughest period of the writing process, I drew strength from a story. The story is of an eighty-seven-year-old laundry woman from Mississippi named Oseola McCarty. In 1995, Oseola gave $150,000 to the University of Southern Mississippi, in her hometown of Hattiesburg. When this meek silver-haired philanthropist made such a generous donation, it caught people's attention mostly because of how she had spent her life: washing other people's clothes. Oseola never had the same opportunities as others. But she didn't complain or blame the world; she just kept washing clothes and saving her pennies so that someone else could have opportunities otherwise not possible. And thank God someone else did. The first recipient of her scholarship was awarded to Stephanie Bullock, a freshman woman from Mississippi. As I read about this story in the paper and saw the picture of Oseola standing next to the young lady who had received her scholarship, I realized even more that had it not been for Oseola McCarty and women like her (such as our mothers, sisters, aunts) the accounts you will read about may not have existed. I was so motivated to continue writing that when someone asked me, "Donna, why are you writing about black women in careers that only a scarce percentage of African-American people ever go into?" I responded, "Because I have been fortunate enough to know twenty-four women who are willing to pick up where Oseola left off." As you read these accounts, I hope you will take from them more than lessons on black women's survival skills in the mainstream, but understand that the next Karen Gibbs, Gail Gross, Judith Aidoo and Brenda Neal may be that young lady from the University of Southern Mississippi. What will this generation of women pass on to her as she starts her career in the year 2000? What would we have done for ourselves and the future?

DONNA M. BALLARD
FEBRUARY 2, 1996

DOING IT FOR OURSELVES

Introduction

"Success?" she says, thinking deeply about the definition. "Well, definitely for the first time in history, we are reaching heights that we have never reached before. No longer are we only in the back offices, but some of us have moved into the boardrooms. You see us at some of the top levels in corporations, and many of us are even running our own businesses. But that doesn't define how successful we have become as professional black women. I think our success is better defined by how we take what we have gained from our experiences, personally and professionally, and use it to advance our presence in the next century. In my mind, that's making sure the generation to follow can benefit from our success and mistakes."

For several months I sat across many dinner and lunch tables, spoke on telephones, visited offices, living rooms, and coffee shops. I listened to two dozen African-American women talk about their careers. Hearing countless messages on what it means to make it as an African-American career woman in the nineties. Their discussions, open and candid, gave greater insight into how African-American women are forging ahead professionally in an ever-changing business world where some question the future of women and minorities in the workplace with the dismantling of anti-bias hiring policies.

On the following pages you will meet what I believe to be some of the most dynamic African-American women in the business world today. This composite includes women in finance, publishing, entertainment, and fashion. It provides an in-depth look at successful women of color in a way that displays the human side of these achievers.

From Wall Street to Hollywood, and ranging in ages from twenty-four to fifty-six, these women represent a reservoir of information as well as provide motivation for young women of all races and backgrounds who aspire for careers in business or to become entrepreneurs. Also, in these interviews, you will meet women who were the *first* in their fields not only as a person of color but as the first woman. While success inside the corporate mainstream is largely the focus of this book, I met with several women who have had to face life after corporate downsizing and restructuring, not so uncommon for hundreds of thousands of Americans. The angst of the nineties has made it far more difficult for anyone to speak comfortably about five- and ten-year plans, but you'll meet women who had to face that all-too-familiar uncertainty of not knowing what will be the "next step." You'll hear how one dealt with the direction of her life after hitting the glass ceiling and how another dealt with her life after being laid off. This book can apply to any field and to anyone who wants to understand what it means to succeed as an African-American woman in business.

In sum, you will meet a number of highly motivating African-American businesswomen who are undoubtedly changing the complexion of the corporate landscape.

Breaking Through the
Last Bastion

4:30 P.M., New York Stock Exchange. A venerable
gray-haired man emerges with a gavel onto a half-
circle platform. A bell rings—marking the end to
another trading day. At the close, the Dow is 4510,
up significantly from the day before. Winners beat
losers two to one. More than 474,000,000 shares
traded on the big board—a record day in the
market. Two hours later, in a post-market-hours
gathering, a group of forty or more professionals
are gathered: bankers, brokers, investment advisers,
analysts—a broad array of industry professionals.
Dressed in well-tailored suits and impressionably
polished, they stand around in an open forum—
trading talk on the events of the day. Moments
later a middle-aged black woman steps to the
center of the room. She is a small-framed woman
with slight flecks of gray near her temples. She
welcomes the crowd and announces a speaker. A
speaker? Not usual for an after-work congregation
of Wall Streeters. But then, this is not a typical
after-trading-hours meeting of market professionals.
The meeting—the Wall Street Network for
Women of Color, a trade organization of mostly
African-American women in financial services and

related fields. The organization's mission—to provide a medium for minority women to share ideas and information relevant to the industry.

TWENTY YEARS AGO IT MAY HAVE NEVER SEEMED possible. But it was happening on a June evening in 1995, for the first time—African-American women from Wall Street banks and financial institutions were gathering to network and share information about their professions. The speaker was Karen Gibbs, an anchor at CNBC. For an hour the group listened as Karen spoke about the early days of her career.

Karen Gibbs

Breaking the News

It's 1:56 P.M. Karen Gibbs is seated under the bright studio lights at CNBC—the Cable News Business Channel. She goes on the air in four minutes. Neil Cavuto, a co-anchor, is seated next to her. They speak for a few seconds about the sharp movement in interest rates during the morning hours. The producer's voice is heard over a speaker at the anchor station—"Ten seconds." A camera swings in. It's now 2:00 P.M. Karen looks up, smiles into the camera, and begins "Good afternoon. I'm Karen Gibbs and this is *The Money Wheel*. At the top of the hour the bond market is rallying on Federal Reserve Chairman Alan Greenspan's inflation outlook. . . . The thirty-year treasury bond is up a quarter point. . . ."

FOR THE AVERAGE 200,000 DAILY VIEWERS WHO watch CNBC, many are familiar with Karen Gibbs— the charismatic ebony woman with a distinctive streak of gray in her hair. Since 1992 Karen has anchored the one-hour financial-news program, covering credit, futures, commodities, and foreign exchange markets activity. Inside CNBC's studio in Fort Lee, New Jersey, I watch Karen during a broadcast. On the moni-

7

tors in the control room Karen appears poised and
calm. "She's a natural," remarks the program's producer, switching to a commercial. The break ends and
Karen resumes. Karen speaks with the grace and ease
of a veteran reporter, although she's been in the business for only a few years. After the program, Karen
speaks over lunch about why she enjoys being an anchor at CNBC. "What's great about what I'm doing
is that when news breaks and you know it's going to
move the markets, it's exciting to get it on the air and
out to our customers. At CNBC, our customers are
the people who have interest in the financial markets.
The energy is very much like that of a trading room,
except in reporting financial news, I don't have to
worry about someone else's money when I go home
like I did when trading."

Before starting at CNBC, Karen was the senior futures and hedging analyst at Dean Witter Reynolds in
Chicago. "My position was to assist the firm and its
clients in hedging their investment risk with futures."
Being in that role introduced her to the financial news
services. "Oftentimes the news-retrieval services such
as Telerate, Knight-Ridder, and Dow Jones called me
for my opinion about what was going on in the market. I prided myself on having a timely and accurate
answer."

The inspiration for Karen to go into a traditionally
male business? She says unbashfully: "I love money—
always have."

"Even as a child I loved playing with coins. It wasn't just money, though. I was fascinated with knowing why things cost as much as they did. As a little girl I'd go into the grocery story and wonder why bacon or coffee was one price this week and a different price the next week. As I got older, I became more curious about complex questions such as why do interest rates set the value of the dollar or why does a crisis in South Africa affect the price of platinum or gold—the answers to those types of questions just always held a big interest with me. And I think it was what pushed me to studying economics in college."

In her senior year at Roosevelt University, Karen took a part-time job at the Chicago Board of Trade (CBOT). She thought working at the CBOT would give her the opportunity to gain practical experience and exposure to the commodities markets. She did gain exposure as well as change history. When Karen started at the CBOT in 1976, she was one of the first African-American women ever hired on the trading floor at the commodities exchange in its 160-year history.

Modest but open, Karen says, "I didn't know if there had ever been an African-American woman to work on the floor before; I just knew what I wanted to do. The board hired me as a board marker.

"Before electronic display boards, there were people who wrote the commodity prices on a large blackboard above the trading floor," she says, laughing (subconsciously acknowledged that she started out before the financial markets became advanced by technology). "And that was my job. Every day for six months I'd stood on a catwalk above the trading floor and wrote twelve-inch chalk figures. Later, I kept a time and sales ledger of the transactions. Afterward, I moved into the pits where I translated the hand signals of the traders. I guess you could say I moved with technology."

Karen admits that being one of the first women of the commodities markets "was very lonely." In a *Wall Street Journal* article, Peggy Obagek, a woman trader at the CBOT in 1976, was cited as saying, "There were so few women at the board that there wasn't even a rest room for women near the trading floor." However, Karen can attest to more than just the gender issue. "When I started, I could count on one hand the number of blacks that were in the business. All were men. And I was always the only black woman." Karen goes on to say that most of the African-Americans she knew when she started have since left the business.

"In general, the commodities business is very tough, and people don't last very long—heart attacks, strokes—people try to make their money and get out. As a result, the turnover rate is high." Outside of the studio, Karen, single, spends time with her family, friends, and pets. "When I am not at work, one of the things I enjoy the most is going somewhere and getting away from it all. I usually try not to stay away from the markets more than three to four days, or I'll lose continuity of the markets. But I'm good for taking a long weekend and just relaxing. In my field, you have to have that balance in order not to get burned out." Burned out Karen is not. In fact, the forty-three-year-old has a lot of energy—positive energy, that is. "Being positive is what has kept me going. I think in order to make it in business you have to have a positive attitude, be able to ignore all the naysayers, because listening to them doesn't get you anywhere. And having that kind of personality has helped me in my position as an anchor. Especially when the markets are going to hell in a handbasket, our viewers want to be assured that everything is okay. And my attitude, I think, does a lot to translate assurance and calmness."

While being positive has helped her move forward in her career, Karen acknowledges that it takes more than just a positive attitude to make it in the business environment. With respect to women and minorities entering her field, the Chicago MBA has this to say about the next generation: "In my opinion, it's still going to be tough in the future. And I say that only because there have been so many challenges on affirmative action. But I don't think we are going back to the fifties and sixties. The genie is out of the bottle— there are too many women and minorities. And the avenues for starting our own businesses are much better. Also, you finally have a level of consciousness that has started to filter to the black community in terms of supporting our own. And I think the potential is absolutely excellent in terms of what we can do businesswise or in the financial arena." While Karen notes the continuing challenges for young African-American men and women, she contends that more opportunities will exist in her field as a result of the changing landscape. "The financial services business has gone so totally global since I entered—twenty-four-hour market trading and a wider range of products to name a few. Take even another example. When I worked at the Chicago Board of Trade, grain commodities represented the lion share of the market. Today financial futures contracts such as interest rate futures* represent more than half of the contracts traded at the CBOT. So things have become much broader. And because of that, I also think there will be more opportunities for people to get a real shot at the business."

---

*Futures are an agreement to buy or sell a specific amount of a commodity or financial instrument at a particular price on a future date.

Benita Pierce

Years Before Diversity

Walk onto the trading floor of a Wall Street firm—
there are no partitions or cubicles to separate the
sea of hundreds: salespeople, traders, and market
analysts who occupy the massive football-field-size
room. Nothing is private, yet there is an absolute
feeling of being anonymous and autonomous.
These market mavens scurry about, buying and
selling, making markets and risking capital. Stand
at the end of a sales-and-trading desk, and a stream
will appear; a stream of crisp white shirts, expensive
ties around the necks of lean and clean-shaven
faces—it's a financial fraternity to some with a
history nearly four hundred years old. Long before
it was common for this fraternity to admit women
and people of color, Benita Pierce had fought to
enter this world.

IT HAS BEEN MORE THAN TWENTY YEARS SINCE BEN-
ita Pierce first walked onto the trading floor of a major
Wall Street firm. When she started out as a corporate
bonds salesperson during the early seventies, only
1.5% of the stock-and-bond sales jobs in the country
were held by blacks, mostly men. While it was uncommon to find women of color in the securities industry

during this period, it was extremely unlikely to find
those who did work in the industry as institutional
sales and trading personnel at a major financial institution, such as banks or investment banks, in New
York. But for nearly fifteen years Benita Pierce sold
corporate bonds to many of the large institutional investors at some of the leading financial institutions.

Today, however, the Boston native doesn't work
for any of the major houses. She is now president and
CEO of B. Pierce & Co., one of the oldest minority-
woman-owned brokerage firms in the country. Benita
left her last position on Wall Street in 1990 to start
her company. On a late Wednesday afternoon, I venture to the lower side of Manhattan to meet with Benita inside her loft/office, which is tucked away on
Greene Street. I want to learn how she had succeeded
in becoming one of the first professional women of
color on Wall Street. I arrive in the middle of a rather
busy morning for Benita. While in the midst of reading
a market report, which is scattered about on her desk,
Benita is speaking on the telephone to one of her accounts. In the open and vast space of the high-ceiling
office, Benita, a tan slight-framed woman, appears un-
phased by the brightness from the ten-foot windows.
Her call is over. She waves me over welcomingly after
we find a quiet spot, away from the noise of the
phones. Early in the conversation, Benita, whose
mother was an artist and father a New England land-
owner, explains that no one in her family pushed her

toward the career she chose. She became interested in working on Wall Street while attending graduate school at New York University, where she was studying for a master's degree in business administration. "I had been the recipient of a fellowship from a major investment bank. After I received the fellowship, two bankers from the firm took me to lunch and gave me a tour of the firm's debt trading floor." This was Benita's first encounter with the fast-moving, intense world of buying and selling securities. Excited by the activity of the shouting and yelling of prices and company names, Benita recalls, "I remember walking on the trading floor and thinking, 'I want to do this more than anything else.' But the reality of finding a position on an institutional sales and trading floor appeared bleak for ambitious Benita. She remained optimistic, though she admitted that from what she saw, there was little encouragement. "Back then you just didn't see any black people working on trading floors. It was definitely unheard of to see a black woman working in the sales areas. But I didn't worry about being the only black woman applying for a position. I was concerned with how do I get in." After graduating from New York University in 1974, Benita began her quest. She decided she wanted to be a salesperson—or account executive—because the "salespeople had more contact with the clients, given their role in maintaining a relationship with the firm's accounts and executing the buy and sell orders for securities. Also, I enjoyed the nature of salespeople more than traders," she explains. "So, I took my résumé to all the investment houses on the Street, but no one would hire me, not even the firm that had given me the fellowship," remarks Benita wryly. "As I went about looking for a job, the response was always the same: 'We'd hire you if you had some experience.' I thought, 'How does anyone get experience if they don't first get the chance to prove themselves?' " As reality began to settle in, she scratched out the idea of working major investment houses, at least for the time being. Instead she turned to the debt sales department of major banks. Benita was fortunate to find a bank that was willing to give her a shot. She recalled her interview with the recruiter, who, she says, "Just thought I was worth giving an opportunity to. He was impressed with my strong interest for a job on the floor. He thought because I was so aggressive, I'd be a good fit for a positon that had become available on the sales desk. (Coincidentally someone had resigned the week prior). However, before he hired me, he needed to know if I could handle the pressure of working on a trading floor. So, he called my parents, who lived on Cape Cod, and asked them if I could deal with a lot of stress. Of course my parents were shocked, but they assured him that I could handle working on a trading floor. And that's how I got the job." But not long after Benita started at the bank, she realized that finding a position was only one of the first bridges she had to cross. It was tough. "I am quite certain that I was one of the first African-American woman on the bank's trading floor," she says. "I know for certain I was one of three women who worked in the department." For Benita, working on the trading floor was a huge test of endurance and of her will to remain a market professional. She leans back in her chair as if she is weighing in her hands two equal masses then says, "I think it was tougher being a woman than being anything else. While I faced obstacles with being a person of color, I would say I dealt with just as many from being a woman," says Benita, turning away momentarily to see where the market last traded for the ten- and thirty-year treasury bonds. Benita's comments ring with great similarity to other women pioneers in the field. Benita describes the environment as gruff and very macho. However, working with men who sometimes had less than congenial natures didn't bother Benita. "It didn't worry me because I knew why I was there. And that was to make money," explains Benita, whose salary was significantly higher than the median $11,000 yearly salary of professional black women in the finance, insurance, and real estate industry in 1982. "I always kept my focus. I knew that everyone wasn't going to welcome me, and I braced myself for it.

"You really had to be as tough as the men to survive. There were no two ways about it. You had to be able to stand up for yourself and not back down. For example, I remember one time a women who worked with me became upset when a trader yelled at her. I told her, 'The next time he yells at you, yell back. Trust me, it works.' And it did," she says with a quick wit. "But understand," she continues, "then the nature of the trading room was very much like that of a locker room. The men shouted and cursed—that was the order of the floor. It's changed a great deal since the early seventies, but then that was just the environment in which we (all women) had to work in. Though after the rough days (when there were shouting matches), someone would say, 'Let's go have drinks' after work, kind of a way to say 'nothing personal.' "

While Benita knew that it was uncommon for her to be in a sales position, she also knew it was even more out of the ordinary to have someone like a mentor. Benita expressed in a "no big surprise" tone that she did not have any internal guidance with respect to her career. "No, I didn't have a mentor. And I don't think we always need a mentor—maybe just someone to give a good piece of advice. I knew a gentleman who gave me a great piece of advice, which helped me throughout my career. He told me, 'Benita, you can't fight every fight. So pick your battles and be prepared to win them.'" Benita recalled how she had used the man's advice in a situation that nearly kept her from being a salesperson. "I had just come out of the training program to find that my new manager thought I'd be better as a clerk—although I was ready to start immediately on the sales desk. Of course, I was not happy about his decision. I asked to meet with him. He told me in a curt tone that he'd only see me for ten minutes. I thought, 'Fine, I won't make this long.' I went into his office and told him that I was trained to be in sales. I didn't mind helping out where I was needed, even if that included the back office. But I expected to be a full-fledged salesperson. He was visibly shocked. He said to me, 'What do you want?' I responded, 'A phone, a desk, and accounts.' He looked at me for a minute and replied, 'How long do I have to think about this?' I returned, 'Ten minutes.' Ten minutes later I had a phone, a desk, and accounts (dormant accounts), but I had accounts! It was up to me at that point to make something happen. But I had to first fight for the opportunity. And I think for most women who have gone anywhere in their careers, that has been the case. There is a constant struggle, it seems, to attain what you want in business, particularly this one. I don't think I would have made it into the position I wanted had I waited for him to give me the chance or for him to decide that it was time for me to stop being a clerk and move into sales. And that's probably the first thing that I'd say to women in business careers: You have to have the inner confidence to speak to people about what it is you want.' "

After two years Benita left the bank. At the other firms she joined in the following years, she says she remained "the first" or "the only black woman" in her department. "It didn't bother me," she explains, "because I knew that it was going to change." By the time Benita started B. Pierce & Co., in 1991, the number of African-American men and women in the securities industry had changed. According to the 1991 Bureau of Labor Statistics, there were 77,000 black professionals.

Although Benita has become her own boss, which keeps her incredibly busy, she says she still finds time to help new professionals in her business. "One word of wisdom I'll commonly pass on to most women entering this field is not to come into it with a really huge expectation of being emotionally gratified. I say this because sometimes we tend to feel that every moment of the work day we will have some 'psychic experience' in our profession. It doesn't happen that way. For many women I have known in this business, they've had to make some hard sacrifices to be where they are, says Benita, who made the decision, earlier in her career, not to marry.

"I'd add also, when starting out in this business, you have to earn your respect by doing a lot of the small jobs and showing that you're hungry for the business. When it comes to accounts, you have to be able to deal with a lot of rejection." Learning to deal with rejection is the hardest part of the business, she says. "I remember how my accounts hung up the phone and said, 'Never call me again in life.' But the next day I called them back and said, 'Now, you didn't really mean that. Listen, I have something interesting to talk to you about. . . . Here's what's happening in the markets. . . . Give me a chance.' It was tough, but everybody goes through that phase. You become better by learning from your mistakes and not repeating them. And that's probably my most valuable piece of advice to younger people starting out."

Benita's advice comes in handy, particularly for herself, because the daily activity of selling bonds to large investors and running a brokerage firm has provided her with a set of new and demanding challenges. "It is a big job running a brokerage firm because the business is very competitive. But I really do enjoy it. I started this firm with my own capital. My decision came after fifteen years of selling bonds for someone else's account. I felt it was time to do it for my own. Also, I want to have a company where 'my' name is on the door. I think it's important that we, as African-Americans, own our own business and make names for ourselves."

Benita *is* making a name herself. B. Pierce & Company is an emerging domestic and international broker dealer with involvement in both the equity and debt markets. The firm's clients include many large asset managers and state pension funds. And although the company, by industry standards, is relatively new, and has not become as common by name as other black-owned investment banks such as Pryor McClendon and W. R. Lazzard, it has been involved in a number of ventures that are quickly gaining it notoriety. "One venture was with a major investment firm for $300,000,000. Now, that is where it becomes a 'psychic experience,' " she says proudly. "I feel the greatest amount of success comes from knowing that my business is growing and helping others aspire to do the same."

And it has. Since Benita started her firm, at least half a dozen other minority-woman-owned firms have cropped up. Investment firms such as the Aidoo Group, Sterling Investment Management, Magna Securities Corp., Cromwell, Miller & Greer Inc.

A Passion for Fashion

The story had all the earmarks of a television mini-drama—a wealthy family, owners of an exclusive clothing chain, sellers of trendsetting fashions, two older sons with lavish lifestyles left the oversight of their father's business. The sons' new ideas and lofty goals lead to upscale store expansions in New York, L.A., and Chicago. Costly changes spawn overruns in the millions, which are speculated as causing financial problems. Japanese partners with huge cash stakes in the company employ what appear to be *Art of War* tactics for rule over a family's seventy-year-old business.

NOT A FABLE. BUT A REAL-LIFE AMERICAN BUSINESS drama that played out in the press. When Barneys, a traditional men's clothing store, filed for bankruptcy in the early part of January 1996, it not only caught the attention of the movers and shakers in the retail industry, but it also made big news on the business pages. Who writes about this kind of drama in the fashion business?

Teri Agins, a senior special writer who has covered the fashion industry for eight years at *The Wall Street*

Journal. Teri writes columns on apparel marketers and manufacturers. The week the *Journal* ran the Barneys story was nothing short of extremely hectic. But covering high-profile merchandisers in the fashion industry is at the heart of why Teri Agins became a journalist. When I spoke to Teri earlier that week, she was under the intense pressure of a deadline (the arch nemesis of a reporter). The story was due to run on Friday, January 12. Teri, far too busy to talk, was on her beat, calling resources and industry insiders—anyone who could give the paper's story a "spin." Not only did the story have to go beyond the mere recitation of facts, figures, and people involved, it had to be timely. In an information-on-demand culture, print journalists are pushed harder to compete with television and news retrieval services. No one waits to read major stories like that of the Barneys bankruptcy on the weekend. By then, such accounts are summarized after a barrage of reports from the prior week.

And by Sunday the story is recapped in Sunday's *New York Times.* The paper ran a two-page article about the retailer. That morning I phone Teri. She's home with a cup of coffee—in a bit of a reverie at the end of an arduous week. She starts with the drama inside the news room. "This week has been just unbelievable! The piece took on a life of its own. Did you read our coverage of the story?" she says, referring to herself and Laura Bird, and Laura Jereski, the other writers covering the story. "Not yet? Pick it up!"

she quips rapidly. (And I did. "Bruised Barneys Seeks Shelter From Creditor" headlined the Marketplace Section of the *Journal*. It was meticulously laid out with the details of the financial woes facing Barneys Gene and Bob Pressman, whose photos appeared in the piece.) Teri continues to talk about how they brought the story together for a few minutes before the discussion turns to her life as a writer. I have never met Teri, but she has a climatic alto voice that suggests the image of sage and veteran reporter—a woman who's known this business all her life. Teri didn't deny that from her earliest memories her life has been propelled in one direction—writing. "As early as a teenager, I had the passion for journalism," she recalled. At fourteen, Teri, the daughter of a first-grade teacher and civil worker, wrote her first fashion column. *Teri's Tips for Fashion Flair* ran eight times a year in the junior high school newspaper. As an English major at Wellsley College, Teri held summer reporting internships at the *Kansas City Star*, a newspaper in her hometown, and the *Boston Globe*. Although her college years were a good training ground for writing, Teri acknowledged she didn't become serious about journalism until graduate school. Teri attended the University of Missouri, where on a Ford Foundation Fellowship she visited Peru for four months—a necessary expedition to complete research for her master thesis on the government control of the press in Lima, Peru. Although Teri had many experiences in journalism, she did not find her first professional job right away. She recalls, "When I graduated, it was the summer of 1977—a few years after President Nixon resigned from the Watergate scandal. Everybody, it seemed, wanted to get a job in journalism. It was a sexy business to be in. Every day you'd turn on the TV and there were people like Barbara Walters reporting on the biggest political story of the century. To find a job you had to have contacts. I think it's still hard now, but at least there are organizations like the National Association of Black Journalists, a trade organization for minority men and women in journalism. Then, such organizations were just coming into existence. I must have sent out 130 letters and didn't get a single response. I eventually found a job with *Daily News Record*, the sister publication of *Women's Wear Daily*. I worked in the Chicago bureau as a reporter—my first full-time job in journalism."

Teri joined *The Wall Street Journal* in 1984, after returning from Brazil, where she lived with her former husband, a Citibank banker whose job relocated him and Teri there. Teri pursued a writing position at the century-old paper on the advice of friend Michael Days, who was a reporter at *The Wall Street Journal* in the Philadelphia bureau. "Mike thought the *Journal* would find my experiences and foreign language background interesting." The *Journal* did find Teri intriguing, after four months of interviews. "I went through a lot to prove I could handle working here," says Teri, who did not have any business exposure. "And for the first three years, it was an uphill battle. I had to learn economics and about the stock market. It was really a challenge in the beginning." Also, Teri worked on a number of beats before she started covering the fashion industry. She explained, "I covered airline companies, small businesses, the U. S. Attorney's office and the courthouse."

After twelve years at *The Wall Street Journal* Teri has proved she is a seasoned pro and expresses a desire to teach journalism later in life. She says one of the first lessons she would teach her students is "in order to be a good journalist, it takes being both cynical and curious—you have to be the kind of person who doesn't accept anything at face value."

What does Teri like most about business journalism and covering stories like Barneys? She summarized by saying, "In any business, even in fashion, there's power, greed, fraud, envy, competition—all of that is drama and people want to read about it."

It's Never Too Late

April stares with an inquisitive smile on her face. She looks at the plate in front of Toni and asks, "Oomie (Swahili for 'mother'), you want this last piece of pie?" before going off to practice her violin. Toni, dressed in a purple and gold lappa, nods affectionately for her to take it. A soothing scent of home cooking perfumes the house. Family photos of four children and five grandchildren at every age line a mantel. A kettle whistles in the kitchen—tea is ready. Toni settles down at her kitchen table and hums a gospel tune. Toni is a full-figured woman with short, curly, salt-and-pepper hair. She has an open and warm face—greeting card picture of a gentle family and church woman, a pillar of the community. But don't underestimate this grandmother.

TONI BANKS, FIFTY-SIX, IS ONE SAVVY BUSINESS-woman. With thirty-plus years in the book publishing industry, a little over twenty of those years at Mc-Graw-Hill Companies, she has become one of the more well-known and admired African-American women in her field. At McGraw-Hill, a Fortune 500 company, Toni is an account executive who sells to

organizations business and trade books used in employee education, training, and management development in the Professional Book Publishing Division.
Selling books has always been something Toni loved.
And on a late December Saturday afternoon, I meet
with her at her home in Brooklyn to learn why. Before
my arrival, Toni had been helping her granddaughter,
April, age twelve, navigate through the World Wide
Web. "My granddaughter just received an E-mail from
a little boy in Taiwan," she remarks proudly as I enter.
Toni takes great joy in her granddaughter's interest in
computers, particularly since she studied Information
Sciences at Fordham University. As her granddaughter
dusts off to practice, Toni relaxes and explains over a
steaming cup of tea how her career started. "Well, I
didn't have the typical career track into the publishing
business," she says, describing "typical" as the twenty-
five-year-old who takes a junior or assistant job after
college and works his or her way up in some publishing company. In 1964 Toni was then a twenty-five-
year-old single parent with four children, who worked
two jobs—as a front desk clerk in a dry-cleaning store
during the day, and a mail sorter (the first woman) in
the New Rochelle post office at night. However, Toni
was interested in giving up her day job at the dry
cleaner to find another. She responded to an ad for a
book order clerk in her community's newspaper in
New Rochelle. The company was Diamondstein's,
then a major New York book wholesaler. "I saw the

ad in the newspaper and thought here was an opportunity for me to work around books. I was raised in
a bookish environment. Being a book order clerk was
a chance for me to be in an environment that I had
grown up in most of my life," says Toni, who credits
her mother for her appreciation of literature. Toni's
mother, a community civil rights activist, raised Toni
and her siblings in one of the first housing projects in
New Rochelle. Though economically deprived, they
did not miss out on many of the experiences affordable to children from families with means. "My mother
gave us a rich cultural upbringing," says Toni.

Toni worked for Diamondstein's for four years.
But in 1968, after relocating her family to Harlem, she
left the company to work for one of its competitors,
Bookazine, presently a thriving book distributor. Like
her experience at Diamondstein's, Toni's job at Bookazine provided her with a vast knowledge about the
book publishing industry. She learned about books
from different types of writers, especially those by African-American authors. And when the owner of Freedom Bookstore, one of the earliest black bookstores
in Brooklyn, came into Bookazine to buy books for its
store, "They influenced me to come work for them. I
had never been employed by black people before," remarks Toni, who anxiously jumped at the chance to
work for a black-owned bookstore. Freedom Books,
no longer in existence, was known throughout the
community. "What made this store so well loved was

that it was one of the only places where many of the
well-known writers and poets such as Nikki Giovanni,
Sonya Sanchez, and Imamu Amiri Baraka (then LeRoi
Jones) could give readings and do book signings," explains Toni like a historian. But the store struggled
financially due to lack of patronage, and Toni was
forced to leave only two years later. "I had four children to raise," remarks Toni, whose husband deserted
them after he came out of the Air Force. Despite the
financial pressure of having to raise her family single-
handedly, Toni still wanted to work for a bookstore
in her own community. In 1972 she worked for the
Harlem Liberty House, a cultural institution that had
grown out of the Jackson Mississippi Poor Peoples Co-
operative. The Harlem Liberty House was more well
known nationally than Freedom Books. "The major
difference between the Harlem Liberty House and
Freedom Books," continues Toni, "was *all* the black
personalities (writers *and* singers, actors, and jazz mu-
sicians) of that period came to the store to buy hand-
crafts produced by the co-op. So you see, it wasn't just
a bookstore." She calls April away from violin practice
to show me a little red tote bag with cloth straps and
sunflowers on the front; the bag, she says, was made
by people in the co-op. "I have had this bag for a lot
of years. It is one reminder that I have from working
there." But the tote bag wasn't the only remnant of
Toni's presence at the Harlem Liberty House. While

working there, she helped establish the first collection of African-American children books. "There were not very many books written for our children back then. But there were a few, and it was such a sense of accomplishment for me to have helped compile a collection of black children's books." While Toni felt she had made a difference in her community by working for the store, the will to remain there was short-lived. Facing the same financial circumstances with the Harlem Liberty House as she did at Freedom Books, Toni had to leave to earn a steadier salary. "Then there was not a huge readership among our people for our own books. Although there were a lot of celebrities coming through the store, overall the demand was not great enough for the store to stay in business. Now that I think about it, it took a lot of guts for me to depend on my own people to pay my salary when I had always been paid by others. It was extremely difficult. I felt saddened to watch another one of our stores struggle to stay in existence. But I did what I had to do," says Toni somberly as she sends April away with the tote bag.

Scanning once again over the local help-wanted ads, Toni found a job—"a switchboard operator at a company bookstore." The company was McGraw-Hill and the job paid $105 a week. Toni took the job working at McGraw-Hill's art deco building in midtown Manhattan. After eight years and several promotions, Toni advanced to operations manager in the McGraw-Hill Professional and Technical Bookstore. "I learned the professional book business working on the switchboard. By listening to the type of books companies ordered when they called, I knew who wanted what," she says cleverly. "After a while the customers would call and say, 'Switch me to Toni, she knows what I'm looking for.' " While Toni took enormous pride in having McGraw-Hill product knowledge, she always regretted not having finished high school. Through McGraw-Hill, Toni went back to school at night and earned her GED. She attended Columbia University's Community Education Exchange Program (CEEP). The program was designed to bring Harlem residents on the campus. "After I dropped out of high school in the eleventh grade to get married and start a family, I didn't have time to go back to school. But after my children got older and I didn't have to work two and sometimes three jobs to support them, I knew I had to finish my education. I was also suffering from the empty-nest syndrome. I never thought it was too late for me to get an education." Once Toni returned back to school, she says, "I realized how much I had missed and how much I enjoyed learning." In 1980 Toni, then in her forties, received an Associate degree in business administration from Elizabeth Seton College. Two years later she returned to Fordham University, where ironically she attended some classes with Susan Taylor, editor-in-chief of *Essence* magazine. Susan Taylor returned to college at age thirty-eight and graduated at age forty-five.

Now, at age fifty-six, Toni Banks has two college degrees, one she says, laughing, "is from the University of Hard Knocks." And while most people may look at Toni as being near the end of a career in the publishing business, she's just beginning. After our chat Toni shows me information about a business she started—an Afrocentric Books Network, a consulting service to writers, publishers, booksellers, and readers. In addition to her business venture, Toni has also hosted a television book program, produced by her oldest daughter, Celeste, on the Brooklyn Community Access Television (BCAT). The program, created as an independent studies project for the completion of Celeste's degree in Media Art, featured authors and well-known publishing professionals. On the program Toni's guests have included two of the top women in the publishing world, Cheryl Woodruff of Ballantine Books and Malakia Adero, editor-in-chief at Amistad Publishing House. "We are all members of Black Women in Publishing. You *do* know about BWIP?" remarks Toni, asking as only a grandmother can. Toni is a longtime member of the trade association which started in 1979 to help women of African heritage gain exposure to the publishing industry. "The organization is much broader now" she explains. "I am on the membership committee of Black Women in Publishing, and one of the things I am so truly proud of is that more of us want to go into this industry. And I don't just mean aspiring editors, but in all the areas such as a literary agent and attorney, art and design, finance and production, marketing, sales, wholesale, and retail."

Wanda Hill

Taking the Lead

On an early summer evening Wanda Hill, forty, looks out of a sixth-floor conference room window as a sea of placid-faced professionals exit the offices on the ground level below. As the rush-hour crowd sifts into the underground passages, Wanda studies the mass of people where some are aggressively pushing their way through the crowd to get home. She returns to her chair where we are discussing success and leadership. The statuesque woman exudes confidence and the attitude of a leader. She speaks in a clear and definitive tone. Her demeanor is not an exaggeration of business etiquette or professional polish but how one must come across when taking the lead. Since Wanda joined The Bank of New York in 1989 via its merger with Irving Trust, her former employer, she has strived and succeeded at becoming a decision maker inside the bank. In 1992 Wanda Hill was promoted to manager in the centralized marketing department at The Bank of New York. Her job is to provide marketing support for the bank's trust, investments, and private banking business.

"ONE OF THE FIRST COMMENTS I'LL MAKE ABOUT leadership is there won't be a memo asking for leaders to step forward. In most cases, you'll have to step up and let your manager know you want the responsibility," says Wanda. Dressed in an elegant blue suit, Wanda leans forward at the conference table and describes how she has had to take a more aggressive stance in the advancement of her career. Not shortly after Wanda moved over to The Bank of New York from Irving Trust, there was an opportunity for her to become the marketing manager of her department. Wanda did not receive the promotion. However, she didn't become bitter. She explains, "I was not well known by the bank's new management, and also because I was viewed as highly competent, but unassertive. I believe management wondered if I would really be able to handle the challenges associated with managing an organization. I was viewed as a strong number two, but they weren't sure if I could effectively manage a group." In the future, however, Wanda would not accept "quiet" and "low key" as reasons for her not moving into higher designation. When the next opportunity came two years later, Wanda made sure the bank's management knew she was ready to take the lead. "I was much more forceful and tactful in asking for the job. Also, I had become better known," she says. Wanda, a graduate of Wesleyan University, in Connecticut, has seventeen years of experience in marketing financial products. And while her successful climb in the marketing field can be attributed to her background and being proactive,

Wanda doesn't evade discussing the common impedi-
ment of women advancing in the workplace, which
often has nothing to do with assertiveness or experience. "Of course, I know there are professional issues
associated with being a woman and a person of color.
And yes, there have been situations where I have been
disappointed. But I didn't stop reaching for the position I wanted nor did I become sidetracked by negative
thinking."

Evidence of that attitude is visible throughout
Wanda's career. Before marketing investment products
at Irving Trust and The Bank of New York, Wanda
managed the marketing communications department
for Calvert Group, a mutual fund company based in
Bethesda, Maryland. One highlight of her tenure at the
Calvert Group was marketing the Calvert Social Investment Fund. In 1982 the company created a mutual
fund that did not invest in companies in South Africa.
"It was a great experience because it was a product I
could totally believe in and enjoy marketing: It took a
stand on important social and political issues and, at
the same time, turned in strong performance results."

While Wanda views her career as a very important
part of her life, she says that her family comes first. A
married mother with two sons, ages twelve and seven,
Wanda expressed, "When I am not working, I spend
most of my time with my husband and sons. It's important to balance the time in the office with family

activities." Wanda is a very active mom. She says she still finds time to check homework and attend ball games and practices.

Wanda has such a fast-paced life both in and outside of the office that I asked her when she has time to herself and how she releases the tensions from both office and home. "God is the best stress reliever there is," explains this Sunday School teacher, who credits her whole family's involvement in the church with her ability to maintain control. Wanda says she also relies heavily on her husband, a tax accountant, for support. "My husband and I share a great deal in common. He is my strongest supporter next to God. And that's critical because you and your husband have to be on one accord, going in the same direction, want the same things out of life, and share in family responsibilities for it to work."

Since my interview with Wanda Hill in 1995, she has been promoted to vice president of sales.

Margot Lee

Finding Balance

Saturday morning—a bright yellow finish line can be seen in the distance. Sixteen cyclists are in a heated rush toward the mark for victory. Only one can cross the finish line first. As anxious onlookers line the side of the park's circumference, they watch and wait to see who will emerge the winner. Cyclist number 23 has picked up some momentum. The lean five-foot-seven frame has a sudden burst of energy to go faster and push harder. Once lagging, now out in front, she leans into the handle bars and presses forward. The finish line is closer. She peddles faster . . . *Shwoosh* . . . cyclist number 23 breaks through the finish line.

THE PRICE OF SUCCESS IS HIGH, SO THE SAYING GOES. And few career women will deny that competing in the fast-moving realm of business is nothing short of running an intense high speed triathlon. Long hours and intense workdays can take their toll on even the most physically fit people. I catch up with Margot Lee shortly after her victory across the finish line. She is still reeling from winning the race that she has trained weeks for. In a fatigued motion, she pulls her bike off the race path and crashes it down on the grass. She takes a minute to catch a deep breath—recouping her energy. Seated on the grass amidst empty water cups and discarded numbers, Margot pulls off number 23 from the front of her jacket. We both stare out into this open terrain of athletes. What immediately strikes me about Margot is that she is a hard-driven goal-oriented woman whose desire to come in first transcends her personal life. Professionally, Margot has achieved a great deal for a twenty-six-year-old. Since graduating from the University of Virginia in 1991 with a degree in finance and French, she has worked for a money center bank in New York as a junior foreign exchange trader and a banker on the capital markets desk at a major Wall Street investment bank. After one year at the investment bank, she was promoted from an analyst to an associate. Margot parallels her accomplishments to the race that has just taken so much out her. "Whether it's a deal that keeps you in the office late or just staying up to par on the job, there's always something that makes you feel as if you're going at warp speed," she says. "It can be draining. That's why I think it is so important to have a balance. For me, part of the balance comes from racing my bike." Ironically, Margot takes comfort from a sport that could not be more of a parallel to her life in the office. But work, like racing, has its rewards for Margot. However, at work the money motivation is not her only incentive for taking herself and her work seriously. "What I've begun to realize is that it is important to have another motivation to work hard. Now, of course, one of the rewards for working hard is to be well paid, but that sometimes just isn't enough. The gratification really comes from something else. I have become more clear-eyed about life and what it means to 'do well.' " Margot admits that getting older has had a lot to do with being less myopic, and much of her balanced view of life she attributes to her parents. Margot was raised in Virginia by a college professor and a NASA scientist. "Both of my parents," Margot says, "are successful and work hard but know there's a bigger picture—family and quality of life are most important." But at one point in her early twenties, she felt every second of her existence should be spent in high gear. "After I graduated from college, being on a super-fast track—having everything before I turned thirty—was all that mattered—I grew up during the big eighties. Now, I'm learning that I can afford to take it a little slow if I want. I'm not saying I want to get married and have two children tomorrow—not to say anything is wrong with that scenario—I just want to learn more about who I am and what I am capable of doing on my own." But don't call Margot a slacker—"My parents wouldn't have it!" she says, laughing. As much as Margot credits her parents for giving her a balanced sense of what's important, they have also been the driving force behind her ambitious goals. "Growing up, my mother and father expected nothing less than the best

from their four children. They never accepted medi-
ocrity. They always expected that we would earn the
highest marks in our subjects and be recognized as
achievers." (Margot, the oldest, says her younger sisters and brother all attended college at the University
of Virginia.) "I think that kind of guidance made the
biggest difference in terms of the confidence I have to
set goals and reach them. I do feel as if I can take on
any job, even if I have never done it before," she says,
holding her number in one hand while sweeping her
braided tresses over her shoulder. If there is any cre-
dence to Margot's belief that balance comes from
standing on her own, proof was what I learned about
her following our talk. Margot left a six-figure position to start her own business, Millennium Consulting,
a consulting company which assists newly formed
companies on financial-related concerns. In only two
months after she left, Margot landed three projects as
a financial consultant to hedge funds. During a phone
conversation, I ask her why the change. Margot has a
lot to say about her newly formed company. But
maybe what best captured why she decided to leave
corporate America and branch out on her own is captured in a short and philosophical answer—a racing
analogy. "I know that I can win someone else's race;
now it's time for me to run my own. And for me that's
the other part of truly finding balance in my life."

Gay Young

Making It Happen

Microsoft wizard Bill Gates predicts life in the twenty-first century as a paperless society where every day for most people will start and end at the touch of a computer keyboard.

I SPOKE TO GAY YOUNG, FORTY, EX–WALL STREET lawyer turned literary agent. Gay not only believes in what Gates says but has built her business, Gay Young Literary Agency, around the future of intellectual property spawned out of the digital information age. Inside her home Gay is seated on a kitchen bar stool sipping a cup of tea. Romaire Beardon prints hang elegantly on her wall and soft music plays. She appears relaxed and unfettered by office work. And why not? She doesn't have to leave her home to work—as Gates predicts will be the case with most people in the future. But Gay is not just another home-based entrepreneur aided with technological conveniences. Gay is a part of what you might call the first generation of information highway attorneys. The caramel-tone woman adjusts her tortoise-shell glasses and explains, "My business specializes in electronic rights, a type of intellectual property, and includes CD-ROM." *Eh?* Not to worry, she doesn't mind that I don't know exactly what that means. When she started her business in 1991, she wasn't sure, either. But after four years Gay has a pretty strong idea and says, "I think in the future there will be a greater demand for reading content on the on-line services that can be accessed through the Internet. I have made a business representing those people who create content—books, magazines, learning guides, etcetera—or want to take existing work, digitize it and transfer it to CD-ROM."

How Gay went from high-powered Wall Street exec to futuristic literary agent, now representing the rights of information-age authors, speaks to the incredible resourcefulness of African-American women who have taken lemons and made lemonade, especially those coping with life after being laid off. She continues, "I was a vice president and senior counsel at Merrill Lynch. I was let go in 1991 in the midst of a downsizing wave on the Street. After I got over the initial shock, I thought, 'Hey! This might be an opportunity.' I always wanted to do something creative but could never bring myself to do it. I think there are many lawyers out there who have a creative side and find little time or motivation to express it. And that was my case. I just took the next raise and moved on.

"However, it wasn't until I was laid off that I was jolted into really thinking about my life and what I wanted to do with the rest of it. I knew I wasn't going to stay in law. So, I spoke to a friend/mentor who was in publishing, Faith Childs, who owns a literary agency in New York. I told Faith I wanted to open a black bookstore. Why not? I love books and I thought owning a bookstore would be a good next thing in my life. Faith was an honest friend, she said to me, 'Honey, you don't have enough money to open a bookstore. I have a thought, why don't you become a literary agent. I hear Charlotte Sheedy is looking for an assistant.' I thought 'literary agent'—okay. I mean, a literary agent has always been my fantasy-type career but never did I think I would become one. So I decided to give it a shot. And I went in to meet Charlotte Sheedy and talk about getting started. Charlotte is one of the most highly respected women in the business. I told her about my background and what I would like to do and she hires me on the spot—as her secretary. In less than two weeks I went from being a well-paid attorney with a secretary to becoming someone else's. It's funny when you think how we become so overconfident once we're in a senior position. I said, 'Sure. I can be a secretary.' I had a secretary and knew what it took to be one. Right?—Wrong. After a week Charlotte calls me in her office," Gay recalls, laughing. "She says, 'Gay, you're no secretary, but you can stay and I'll teach you how to be a literary agent.' And that was my first introduction to the business. For me, it was wonderful being there because I learned from the ground floor about publishing, how literary agents work, and I just completely got a sense for the business. I viewed the year I worked there as an intense graduate program, the same way people see Harvard Business School or maybe the mail room at Creative Artist Agency (CAA).

"While I was working for Charlotte Sheedy, I went to a seminar given by Apple computer for people in publishing. Apple did an in-depth introduction on electronic publishing—it was a demonstration—Arthur's Teacher's Trouble, a very sophisticated learning guide that has done so well on the market. As I'm sitting there watching this demonstration, I'm totally amazed by how technology is being used to educate and entertain us. I had worked on Wall Street with storing documents on CD-ROM. But I never knew that you could take text, pictures, and sound and store on a CD-ROM in an educational or entertaining way. While I'm watching this whole presentation, I'm thinking, 'This is definitely the future.'

"I decided that here is where I wanted to make my mark. In the literary business, you try to find that niche where you feel you can make a name for yourself. With some literary agents it is science fiction, with others it's children books, and so forth. And I thought, 'Why not here; working with electronic rights and people who have existing material they want transferred to CD-ROM and the Internet? What I didn't realize at the time was that even though people are talking a lot these days about the digital revolution and where it's going, all of this stuff is still very new. And in the beginning, starting my new media business was very tough because the business overall is still in its embryonic stage. I guess, that's the first thing I'd say to women venturing out there: Make sure there's a real market for your business. But since I've started I have seen the business grow, and that is so exciting because so much has changed in just a short time. I think owning my own business is the best thing I could have done; I know I'm building a business that is on the cutting edge of technology. My regret, not having done it sooner. In retrospect, I think I was in the wrong kind of law."

Lydia Payne

One Step at a Time

From a Dean Witter office on the sixty-fourth floor in the World Trade Center, Lydia can see uptown, to the end of Manhattan. The distant horizon is more than just a picturesque view of her vantage point. It is somewhat symbolic of where she saw herself earlier in life. Her voice fades out for a second. She clears her throat, then returns a second later in a reflective tone. "You can overcome by moving on and advance by looking ahead. I never viewed myself as limited by anything and never accepted a defeatist attitude. Never."

LYDIA PAYNE IS SPEAKING FROM TWO POINTS OF view. First, from the career woman who made her way to the top of the upper echelons of corporate management as director of advertising at Dean Witter, the seventy-year-old brokerage firm, and second as the once young mother who refused to abandon the prospects of what an education held for her. After a morning of conference calls with Dean Witter's Chicago-based advertising agency, Lydia takes a few moments to discuss her thoughts about moving up the corporate ladder and why she feels that success is truly a "step-by-step process."

"I think if there's anything that I have learned over the years it is that there isn't just one thing that makes your career, it is an amalgam of things. I have held several jobs throughout my career. In some, I had to take the junior position, but I realized that you have to view each position you assume as a learning opportunity and stepping stone to something better, even if it seems as if you're taking a step backward."

After the birth of her son, André, Lydia, at age seventeen, pursued college. "My mother raised my sisters and me with the belief that we were no less than anyone else. Even during an era when it was a stigma to be a single young woman with a child, she never let me feel limited by what I could do." Lydia attended Hunter College in New York, where she grew up. Her major was music/piano. Following graduation, Lydia's goal was to teach secondary school in the New York City Public Schools, but a fiscal crisis during the mid-seventies lead to cutbacks, and Lydia was forced to choose another career path. At twenty-three, she took a job as a new accounts supervisor at Edwards & Hanly, a small New York-based regional brokerage firm. "I don't know what interested me in going to a brokerage firm. But I did and after I got into the job and cut my teeth on the brokerage business, I found I liked it and wanted to stay." Lydia moved a year later to Shearson Hayden Stone, a larger regional firm, where she worked as a junior commodities trader. Working in commodities put her in the fast-paced frenetic world of trading, but she says, "The stress of the job was more than I was cut out for. I just realized it wasn't for me. I knew I wanted to do something else but wasn't sure. So my manager, who was a woman, suggested that I consider advertising—since I had a background in music, there might be a fit with doing commercials. She offered to introduce me to one of her friends in the advertising industry." Through the woman, Lydia found a job at UniWorld Group, the second largest black-owned advertising company. At UniWorld Group, Lydia worked as an administrative assistant, earning less than she had as a junior trader at Shearson Hayden Stone. Undeterred by the fall in her wages, Lydia focused on her first mission inside the advertising company—learning the lay of the land. "I think when you start out in any company, you go in learning as much as you can about the business, and that was my objective. I didn't mind that I had to take a job as an administrative assistant, because I believe that in many instances that is the only avenue for women to get our feet wet in a company. Fortunately, I reported to the top woman at the agency, who took me under her wing and opened up the world of advertising to me."

"It was a valuable experience for me because the company was small and I got the chance to touch and feel almost every aspect of the business—it was a world apart from what I had done at Shearson, but I was open to trying something different." Lydia found that she enjoyed advertising and after a year moved to a larger advertising agency, DeGarmo & Co.

"At DeGarmo," Lydia continues, "I developed a wider set of skills and expanded my understanding of the advertising business. There, the creative director also took me under his wing. I expressed a desire to learn how to make television commercials and he suggested I go to the School for Visual Arts." Lydia took the suggested courses, and by her second year she was promoted to assistant television producer.

After four years at DeGarmo, Lydia says she got a call one day. It was a head hunter looking for someone with experience in advertising and financial services—his client was Dean Witter." In 1981 Dean Witter employed Lydia as a regional advertising coordinator. In that position she handled advertising requests from the firm's local branch offices on the West Coast, Pacific Northwest, Southwest, and Midwest. Over fifteen years Lydia advanced three times from assistant vice president, advertising in 1985 to vice president, marketing service manager in 1990, and in 1995 to director of advertising. "It was somewhat ironic that I would go back to a business that I started in, but my experience was an indication and lesson that things don't happen in a direct path. I think as women we often expect everything to fall into place in a very specific organized way."

"I've always said don't self-select yourself out of anything. Had I not been willing to take the job at the UniWorld Group, I would have never learned about the advertising business or even known that it was a fit for me. You have to capitalize on what you know and look at each job as a stepping stone to something better. What also helped my career was reading up on what skills it takes to do my job. When I went to the creative director at DeGarmo and asked what do I need to do to get into television production, he told me to take some copywriting and production courses. That may not have been what I wanted to hear, but I did it and when I did, he delivered to me. I also apprenticed with a senior producer who taught me a lot about television production—even how to conduct casting sessions."

Now as vice president and director of advertising at Dean Witter, Lydia is responsible for maintaining the integrity and reputation of the firm through its corporate advertising programs, which must meet the combined approval of the Director of marketing, national sales, Dean Witter's president, Chief Operating Officer and the Chief Executive Officer. As the "keeper of the corporate image," Lydia explains, "my responsibilities spanned beyond advertising. I am in the role of mediator, translator, and facilitator between Dean Witter and our various advertising agencies, which affords me the best of both worlds (advertising and financial services)." Lydia credits

Dean Witter with giving her the real chance to put in practice the skills that she has acquired at every interval of her career. Now that Lydia has moved up to one of the most senior positions at the firm, reporting directly to the executive vice president and director of marketing, she says, "My learning doesn't stop. I have just earned my J.D. from New York University's Law School. One of the challenges I'd say of being in this position is that even with many years of experience there is still so much more to know. My continuing challenge is to demonstrate a capacity to learn."

Sandra Stevens

Programmed for Success

When Sandra Stevens took a temporary job at Fox Video Inc. in the film library in 1992, she knew she wasn't going to catalog photos for the rest of her life. "My goal was to become an executive," she says. Sandra sent her résumé to the personnel department at Twentieth Television. Within a couple of days she got a surprise response. Her résumé had caught the attention of an executive at the network, and shortly after she was hired as the assistant to the senior vice president for Business and Legal Affairs. Within two years Sandra Stevens became the manager of current programming at Fox Broadcasting Company. Since Sandra took over her current position in 1994, she shares the responsibility of working on each episode of an assigned drama and/or comedy series to keep them on the air. With hit series such as *Living Single*, *Martin* and *New York Undercover* to her credit, this thirty-something female executive is definitely programmed for success.

SANDRA STEVENS'S SUCCESS STORY MAY SOUND more like the Cinderella tale for young aspiring Hollywood executives, but in truth the twisting path she took before getting a break in the entertainment industry is more a story of perseverance, compassion, and positive thinking.

I spoke with Sandra one afternoon. The raspy voiced Detroit native began our conversation expressing that she always wanted to be in the entertainment industry. After Sandra graduated from the University of Pennsylvania with a degree in international relations, she pursued a law degree from the University of California at Berkeley. Her focus was entertainment law. "My mentors were lawyers. I decided I would follow in their footsteps. Although I didn't want to practice law, I knew having that ability to think critically would help me in the long run," Sandra explains. While law school provided Sandra with the skills to analyze, it wasn't a substitute for the action of being around celebrities. At Berkeley she became involved with numerous benefits which drew big names in the music and entertainment world. She even helped organize a benefit to make the birthday of Dr. Martin Luther King, Jr., a national holiday. If social planning wasn't enough, Sandra had taken an interest in photography. She worked as an assistant to a high-fashion photographer. However, irony ran parallel to her short-term photography job. "While visiting Atlanta, I had dinner with some friends in a restaurant. A woman approached our table and asked me if I was a model." Sandra, a striking five-foot-ten beauty who had always seen herself as the ugly duckling of the family, responded half seriously, "Yes, I am." The woman wrote down her number and gave it to Sandra. "It turned out to be a model scout from fashion giant Oscar de la Renta," she recalled with a bit of a chuckle.

"I think life presents you only a few great opportunities, and this was one of them."

At twenty-five, Sandra left law school in her third year, to the complete shock of her family, and launched an international modeling career. "The chance to model was truly a fantasy come true, and I took full advantage of it. Still, I wanted to go into the entertainment industry. I had no plans of going back to law school, but my intentions were clear about entertainment."

Despite clear intentions, it seemed the entertainment industry would have to wait, at least for four years. Sandra went all over the world, from New York to New Zealand, as a print and runway model—she became the first African-American woman on the cover of a magazine in New Zealand. After the novelty and luster of modeling wore off, Sandra refocused on her ultimate goal. "I knew I wasn't going to model forever. It was just something I thought of as exciting, and it was. However, the sign for me to stop modeling came while I was in Los Angeles. My photograph portfolio was stolen, and I took it as an omen and decided to move on," she says spiritually.

Sandra, then twenty-nine, returned to Los Angeles and her family to find life was not pretty and glam-

orous on the streets of South Central. In 1991 the
words *drive by* had become synonymous with gangs
and gangs synonymous with *black* and *Hispanic*. Sandra, jolted by the infectious drugs and crime in her
community, felt an inner call to do something. She put
aside that delicate nature of a woman who could so-
phisticatedly strut down a runway and rolled up her
sleeves to get involved. She moved back into her community and spent a year helping troubled teens. Sandra had become so active that her efforts garnered her
the Vision of the Community Award given by the MJB
Transitional Recovery Center, a community support
agency in Los Angeles. However, after a year she felt
her real career plans had been put on hold long
enough.

She took a temporary job at Fox. Her main con-
cern, she says, "was just getting my foot in the door."
Up until this point fate, good looks, and smarts had
pushed her in one direction, which in Hollywood is
often a winning combination for success. However,
for Sandra to get into a decision-making role—behind
the camera—she knew that she had to make things
happen. As the assistant to the senior vice president of
Business and Legal Affairs at Twentieth Television, she
says, "I had full reign to learn everything about the
business. I never took the opportunity for granted."
While working close to some of the top powers at Fox,
Sandra took evening courses at UCLA's extension
school in film and television. "My goal was to become

an executive. So I had to learn how to think like one, and that meant knowing the right questions to ask. I took evening classes while working during the day. I am a firm believer that you have to research and prepare. Often, I'll meet young people who want to break into the industry, but they have not prepared." The preparation and homework paid off for Sandra. After two years in the assistant position, Sandra was ready for the next move. She went to her manager and asked, "What's next?"

"I think the key is to get as close as you can to a person who can help you achieve a goal and ask them a question you need a 'yes' answer to about your aspirations." Presented with the position of manager of current programming, Sandra knew it was the break that she had been waiting on.

While Sandra's route to success had a few turns, she always remained clear of the goal. She adds, "That was the key, even when it didn't seem like I knew what I wanted to do. I once heard writer Toni Cade Bombara give a speech to the graduating students at UCLA. She said, 'If your intentions are clear, the universe will accommodate itself to help you.' I believe that!"

Now, the highly spiritual and deeply grounded Hollywood executive spends her days dealing with producers and studio and network executives. One of the big highlights of her career is working with industry professionals who are committed to making positive programs about African-Americans and Hispanics. "It's been very inspiring to work with people like Yvette Lee Bowser, producer of *Living Single*. In the future I want to get on the development side and work to produce programs, too."

Gail Gross

Being Strategic

Inside the ground-floor office at The Bank of New York, one of New York's oldest banks, I meet with Gail Gross, thirty-seven, a vice president in the Training and Development Department. After a day of coordinating a sales skills and product knowledge learning session for the branch's employees, Gail is a little more than tired. But this self-taught professional trainer is used to the hectic pace of handling myriad tasks. I enter her office as she is thumbing through messages. She notices me as well as the time on the wall. Gail has another meeting to attend outside of the bank. A slender woman who still has her size-four figure from her days of modeling, Gail is quick on her feet as she packs her briefcase. She invites me to attend. "We can talk on the way," she says as we exit the building.

SHE BEGINS OUR INTERVIEW IN A CAB RIDE THROUGH the city. "For most of my career, I have had to be strategic to get the positions I wanted. And this is something I always share with the young women I mentor from the INROADS and Columbia University's OD programs. I tell them, 'Make sure you market your skills properly, because you are your only prod-

uct.' " Gail credits strategic self-marketing as having
played a major role in her road to success. She even
recommends a self-marketing career guide, *Marketing
Yourself*, by Dorothy Leed, as an excellent book for
women entering the business world. She continues to
describe how it has helped in her career. "I worked
for a number of different banks, and I gained a different set of skills from each of them. As I moved on,
I leveraged off of those skills to advance my career.
Whether it was commanding a higher salary or an opportunity to learn an area of the training field I had
not been exposed to, I always used my skills from one
position to sell myself in another."

Gail started her career as a training professional in
1979. Formerly an assistant buyer for fashion shoes at
Abraham & Strauss, Gail decided after a year to transfer into a more employee-oriented side of the department store. "I thought training fit more closely with
my background. Plus, I didn't study that hard at
Brown University to look at shoes all day long." From
Abraham & Strauss, Gail moved to financial services
training. Within a decade Gail made four career
moves. One position involved training and traveling
internationally (which added to Gail's repertoire of
skills). However, by the end of the eighties Gail's
fourth career move landed her back at the first bank
she worked for in 1980. "During the merger between
the first bank and the fourth bank," Gail notes, "I
learned why you should never burn bridges." Having

left on good terms, Gail was in the position to contact key players at the acquiring bank to ascertain the bank's training expectations. With this information in hand, she knew how to market herself and her staff's capabilities. Again, being strategic was instrumental in securing her position in the merged environment.

By the end of our conversation, the cab has stopped. We're on the Upper East Side of Manhattan, in front of an upscale women's boutique called Carlisle. Inside the opulent fashion house a small assembly of women begins to form. Gail slips past the beveled doors and starts to greet the early arrivals. Gail is the host of a benefit for the Girls' Vacation Fund (GVF), a sixty-year-old New York-based charity which sends some of New York's most underprivileged girls to camp for a summer. Being involved in the charity is a big part of Gail's out-of-office life. And that's clear from the positive energy she exudes after having spent an entire afternoon in meetings. After the function ends, we're back in a cab headed to Grand Central. Gail settles into the backseat of the cab and reflects on all of the day's events. "This is the other aspect of my life that is as important to me as my work." Gail, a single career woman, adds, "Often, it's said that we (career women) opt for the fast track in corporate America instead of raising families. I don't agree with this thinking. I believe there are plenty of women, like myself, who are involved in raising families although we don't have children. Through my involvement with the GVF, I am able to send young girls, a large number of whom are African-American, to camp. And to me that's extremely important because so many of our children are trapped day-to-day inside the city and never have a chance to get out and breathe clean air or just be in a setting where there is no violence or drugs." Growing up in Annapolis, Maryland, Gail says she has a strong appreciation for clean surroundings and the positive impact it can have on the self-esteem of children. She continues, "Of course, volunteering my time to the GVF and the Catholic Big Sister Program, my first volunteer endeavor, doesn't fully equate to rearing a child, but I think it does contribute to saving children whose parents can't afford to. And if I had to measure my success, I would definitely include my impact and input to both organizations on my list of achievements." Once again the cab meter stops. Inside the train station Gail sifts through her briefcase and hands me a Girls' Vacation Fund brochure and her business card. Her train is about to depart. But she gets in one last comment before she leaves: "You should really think about getting involved."

Carla Harris

No Limitations

Resting on a credenza on a trading floor desk are a multitude of Lucite tombstones. Inscribed on them are the terms deal underwritten by Morgan Stanley & Co., Incorporated. Such deal toys comes from well-known retailers, apparel manufacturers, transportation and health care companies. Since 1991 Carla Harris has been a highly visible player on a team of bankers who assisted many of these companies in their initial debut into the markets and helped others raise significant capital in the public equity markets.

On the upper West Side of Manhattan I am having dinner with Carla, an even-keeled banker who's found an hour to talk after an incredibly busy week of working on three deals. The thirty-three-year-old Harvard MBA is a vice president at Morgan Stanley & Company in New York, where she has spent the past five of her nine years in the Equity Capital Markets Division, responsible, in part, for developing the pricing, marketing, and distribution strategies for some of the equity deals underwritten by the firm. Being in this position makes Carla only one in a handful of African-American women in senior positions at major firms on Wall Street. Carla doesn't dispute that it is a challenge for women and people of color. However, she views herself as her primary limitation in terms of where she can go. Very much an educator and motivator on what it takes to succeed in business as a woman of color, Carla has turned our conversation into a teacher-student discussion on limitations. "Look," she says, pushing aside her plate, engaging more into the discussion. "It's tough in business *period*. In order to survive you have to believe that you are your own limitation while remaining cognizant of the enormous obstacles that will, no doubt, be presented in your path. And I work in the type of business where no one gives you anything; you have to step out there and assume it is all yours." Assuming "it's all yours," Carla explained, "means being confident enough in yourself to go after the tougher assignments in your career and knowing that you can do the job and are capable of doing it correctly. Taking on those challenging assignments are often what makes you stand out. Many times you won't be told what they are. And that's another part of assuming 'it's all yours,' figuring out what will be most helpful to the clients and your teammates and doing it." Most people are sometimes apprehensive, though, about taking on such leadership positions because the outcome of making an independent decision is not always clear or spelled out. But Carla, who has a take-charge, no-excuses persona, says, "I've always felt that it is easier to beg for forgiveness than it is to ask for permission. As African-Americans, we often fall into a habit of asking permission to do everything. Whereas others just do and assume that they can. It is a strange lesson for us to learn, especially as African-American women, that assertive, powerful leaders of any color or sex do first and ask questions later. When you ask someone if you can do something, you are giving them the opportunity to tell you no, even when they might not have the real authority or power to tell you no. If you have thought about a course of action or dialogue thoroughly and you have checked it with your 'power source'—mine is God—and is the best possible action plan, then execute it. If you were wrong for having gone forward and you are reprimanded, you can always say, "I'm sorry, but I thought it was the best course of action," but you will already have moved that much further ahead and would have learned from your actions. But in making any decision whether alone or as part of a team requires using good judgment and using the wisdom of others—consulting that power source I mentioned earlier. It was something I understood very early during my college career that I did not nor could I have made the strides and achievements that I have made without God. Developing a strong spiritual base became an obvious necessity during my freshman year at Harvard and it is something that I have continued to nurture and rely on ever since.

There is no major decision that I make in a deal without calling on my power source for confidence and
courage sometimes to step into uncharted territory.
With the faith that He will never steer me wrong, I
have the faith and the confidence that I will always do
a stellar job in whatever I endeavor. I also can have
the confidence to look a client in the eye and tell him
or her that I am giving the best advice." While Carla
continues to explain how she's dealt with some of her
most challenging assignments in her career, she adds
that she's definitely not alone in her thinking. Most
business professionals have a similar philosophy on
being a go-getter, and sometimes aggressive people
clash in business. "It is an intensely competitive world,
Professional America, and you must always be prepared for someone to challenge you or to put themselves in competition with you. When someone else
has decided to be in competition with you, they will
try to undermine your self-confidence and make you
feel less than you really are or that you can do less
than you know you can. Whenever you start to feel
that way, remember that you are giving someone the
power to make you feel that way and that you have
the power to stop the negative process and rescind the
permission for someone to treat you that way." Another way in which Carla has kept control of her
career is managing how others view her as a professional. "Perception is the co-pilot to reality. I have
learned through observation and experience that how

people perceive you directly impacts the reality of how they deal with you. It is very important that you decide early on what you want people to understand or know about you and then you must act in accordance with that objective and actively manage people's perception of you to the best of your ability. It is very true that you cannot control one hundred percent of what people think of you, but you can control your behavior and what you allow them to see and know."

Carla says these principles have been very much a part of her life even in college, during the time which she first discovered that she was suited for a career in investment banking. In Carla's second year at Harvard she was accepted into the Sponsors for Educational Opportunity (SEO), a New York-based organization that places minority students for a summer at many of the top investment banks, consulting, and accounting firms. In 1982 SEO placed Carla with Blythe Eastman Paine Webber, then the investment banking arm of Paine Webber. Working in public finance, Carla quickly gained a passion for the business. Carla described herself as "a self-professed adrenaline junkie.

"For me, the intensity and speed at which everything happens just seem to fit well with my personality and energy level. Up until my sophomore year, I had gone to Harvard with dreams of becoming a lawyer. However, it wasn't until I spent a summer in banking that I learned it wasn't necessarily lawyers who made the world go around, it was businesspeople."

But Carla isn't all work. "When you work hard, you must play hard to achieve balance in your life." The native Floridian sings R&B, jazz, and gospel, works out, and is heavily involved in her community. She is known and respected for giving motivational speeches to collegiate and graduate school women. At the Spelman College 1993 Convocation, Carla delivered a powerful and moving speech on "Playing to Win." The closing words offered to the ladies of Spelman best embodies all of the rules that Carla has played by in order to become a successful African-American businesswoman. She said, "It's ultimately about not accepting complacency, not accepting a mediocre grade or reputation when you have the talents to do better, it's about not accepting being overlooked for a promotion for a reason that makes no sense or for no reason at all, it is about letting people know and think that you are serious about everything you do, that you expect to be consulted about decisions, especially when they directly involve your life, your family's life, or your career, it's about making sure that you are always in the counted few who get recommended for scholarship, who get on the short list of political appointments, who get a shot to vie for a new position."

Sole on Africa

By midmorning a small band of men are standing in a open room buying and selling stocks. They speak with a foreign accent while scribbling numbers on tickets and watching the gyration of market prices. This is a newly formed stock exchange in an emerging country, but it is not in Latin America or the Pacific Rim. This market activity is taking place in one of the least likely of places.

ON THE WESTERN COAST OF AFRICA IN GHANA, THE Ghana Stock Exchange has opened. To some, it may be far-fetched to watch publicly held companies trade in a once Socialist land. However, to Judith Aidoo, thirty-three, president of The Aidoo Group, a merchant bank specializing in African capital markets, the country of Ghana has a burgeoning economy and is just one of the many African nations that are capable of operating viable financial markets. And Judith should know. In 1989, at age twenty-six, she advised the Ghanaian government on the establishment of its exchange as a mechanism for selling state-owned assets to the public. She wrote the feasibility study for the exchange, which is widely referred to as the "Ai-doo Report" and used as a case study for the development of stock exchanges in other countries. I speak with this twenty-first century woman who has become one of the most highly sought after advisers and experts on African finance. On a seven A.M. call Judith sounds far more alert than most people shortly after daybreak. Aside from the fact that she is an early riser, it's the afternoon in Africa, where she has spent the past six months. Only a few days back in the States, at her home, Judith's schedule is already filled with meetings, but fortunately for me, she's found a little time to talk about how her company came into existence. Judith explains how a vacation to a country that she had not seen since her teens led her to where she is today. "I hadn't been back there [Ghana] since my days of boarding school," remarks Judith. "In traveling to the region I met with some people who worked with the International Finance Corporation (IFC). I learned that there was a desire to develop a stock exchange. Out of a personal interest, I offered my time away from work to assist them in making the venture a success." Then Judith worked in New York for Goldman Sachs & Co., in the Fixed Income Sales and Trading Division. She structured financial instruments and investment portfolios for institutional investors. At the request of the IFC, Judith used her personal vacation time to join a small team of financiers who visited Ghana in May of 1989. "However," Judith

continues, "by some strange twist of fate the leader of
the team did not come. And I, a junior person, was
responsible for leading the presentation to the government. There I am standing in front of the minister of
finance discussing the establishment of the exchange
and how I would lead the mission," she says with a
laugh. Judith proved that she could carry the ball and
move a nation of seventeen million people closer to
Western capitalism. After her success with the Government of Ghana, she was quickly called upon by the
World Bank, the United Nations, and other countries
such as Uganda, Nigeria, Kenya, Zimbabwe, Zambia,
Mozambique, Lesotho, and Gambia on similar fronts.
In 1990 she joined a World Bank delegation that trav-
eled into Africa to hold a conference on the development of African capital markets. "It was such an
exciting experience for me. We're talking about advis-
ing the heads of countries, ministers of finance—this
was really high-level finance!" explains Judith. However, it became clear to Judith, who had used up all
of her vacation time traveling to Africa that she needed
to start her own company if she wanted to focus solely
on Africa. In 1991, at age twenty-eight, Judith established The Aidoo Group, an American-based company
with offices in New York and Virginia. While the vision to start The Aidoo Group came from almost "di-
vine intervention," says Judith, a Rutgers College and
Harvard Law graduate with four years of experience
at Goldman. She contends, "I didn't just jump out

there. I had something to sell (experience and education). Plus I spent two years making the important
contacts with people at the IFC and the World Bank.
Conceptually, that's important for anyone who wants
to start a business. I think the market will support you
if it believes that you can win. But first, you've got to
have something to sell." Now The Aidoo Group sells
more than financial advisory services to nations in Africa looking to set up stock exchanges. "We've grown
significantly," she adds. "The Aidoo Group also assist
companies in Africa to raise capital through issuance
of securities. In addition, we have started Aidoo
Group Asset Management (AGAM); we invest in what
we believe are undervalued assets in Africa." Being
one of the first asset managers to target African markets exclusively is indeed an accomplishment but pales
in comparison to her involvement with the Eastern
and Southern Africa Bank for Trade and Development, also known as the PTA Bank. Judith was the
financial adviser in the establishment of an innovative
securitization program for some African trade receiv-
ables. In a proud tone she describes what this deal
meant not only to her but to the future of Africa. "If
I never do another deal in my life, the PTA Bank deal
is one that I think defines what we set out to do with
this business. We made history for both Africa and
ourselves as investment bankers, by raising U.S. $500
million for African exporters at the cheapest interest
rate in the Free World. This was no less than financial

alchemy. We were able to repackage export loans from African countries considered among the riskiest in the world and wrap them with an innovative credit enhancement that transformed the credit risk of the deal to investment grade. In fact, the financing vehicle that we created for the deal, the PTA Bank Funding Corporation, is the only purely African-related financing structure that has ever, and I mean *ever*, earned a short-term credit rating of A1+ with Standard & Poor's and F1+ with Fitch Investor Service. With these ratings African exporters could effectively borrow hundreds of millions of dollars at largely the same interest rate as the best corporate names in America. This has never been done before, and I thank God that we were able to do it because cheaper capital makes for cheaper exports, and cheaper exports lead to greater world demand for African products. And this, after all, is at the root of future African growth and development." With such a phenomenal accomplishments for The Aidoo Group, it may seem as if Judith knew everything about how to run a successful business the moment her company took root. On the contrary, says Judith, who admits to not having a business plan when starting her company, "There were a lot of lessons I had to learn in order to run a business." For starters, Judith says she had to adapt to being away from her family and friends most of the time. "I am in Africa about two-thirds of the year. It was not something I consciously considered when I started, but

I accept it as a function of running a successful company." While time invested in a growing business is an important factor for any entrepreneur, it is a second consideration to having the capital to start a business and keep it going. Judith launched The Aidoo Group with her own money and knows the insecurities that one can face when venturing out of the financial comfort zone of a well-paying job. "It was scary at first. But I realized when starting out, I didn't need a large amount of capital to get my company off the ground, but I did need enough to stay alive or 'stay in the game.' I believe that's the key for most people in business. You need to have enough money to stay alive—meet your overhead costs. If you can stay alive, then you have a greater chance of positioning yourself to get the type of business projects that will help your company grow. In learning this lesson, my entire concept of money has changed, as I think it does with most people that are in business for themselves. I think whatever quantum of money gives you comfort today will shift over time; it is definitely not static. I realized that life consists not in the abundance of things I possess, but rather what I am able to do with what I possess." And maybe it is this levelheaded philosophy that has kept Judith and The Aidoo Group going strong. Industry respect and recognition have merited Judith an appointment by late Secretary of Commerce Ron Brown to the U.S.–South Africa Business Development Committee, along with articles in *Forbes*, *The Wall*

Street Journal, and *Black Enterprise and Financial Times* about The Aidoo Group, which by its fifth-year anniversary had been involved in nearly seven billion dollars in transactions. However, Judith takes all of the accolades in stride as she looks forward to the next five years. She says, "I absolutely enjoy what I am doing. The Aidoo Group is helping, in part, to chart the course of nations in Africa. Also, it's profitable and I get the chance to play at a very high level, a level that had I remained in the States I might not have reached. I feel as if I found something that is uniquely my own. It feels almost natural that I can also serve as a bridge between Africa and America; it is just a part of who I am," explains Judith, born in Washington, D.C., to a Ghanaian father and American mother. "That reminds me of something I once heard my friend, Samuel Akainyah, say at the opening of his art gallery: 'Everybody has something that is uniquely their own. I think that the challenge for everybody is to find out what it is and do it.' And I think I've found what is uniquely my own," says Judith as she departs apologetically to take a business call from London.

Thinking Global

It's 6:45 A.M. For the first few minutes of the morning, I am seated next to Shahri Griffin, international bonds salesperson at BZW Securities, Inc. Shahri stares into a computer screen displaying boxes with a maze of numbers—interest and exchange rates from different European countries. Her eyes quickly scan the pages for developments in the overseas markets. When asked what she does, Shahri thinks briefly as she searches for a not-so-textbook answer. "Well, primarily I sell foreign bonds (bonds issued by non-U.S. companies and governments) to institutional investors such as hedge funds, money managers and banks." Our talk is disrupted for a few moments. A colleague has taken a seat next to Shahri. They talk for a second about the commute into the office. As we're seated there, a message scrolls across the bottom of the screen: "German Bundesbank cut interest rates." The few minutes of morning quiet are over.

TO WATCH SHAHRI ON A DAY WHEN NEWS HAS IM-pacted the financial markets in a big way is like watching a battery-operated doll in motion. The phones, which were once quiet, are now busy. Shahri hits one button—direct line to outside accounts. She yells to a guy down the desk, "Jack, line one." She hits another line, it's her account—a fund manager needs a price on 10 million bonds he wants to sell. It's clearly the start of a busy day in the markets. Shahri, conscious that we have not finished, turns to me and says, "Stay there, I'll be right back!" The diminutive woman slips off to get a price from one of the traders. Seconds later Shahri returns and grabs a phone to dial back her account. Half a minute has passed. In anxious gesture she shrugs her shoulders. "The market is moving," she mutters. She's got him on the phone. Then, in a language only spoken by market people, Shahri begins, "John, I'm back. Okay. We bid 98 for 10 million." She gives an explanation while looking at the bond math monitor about why her account wants to sell the bonds at that *level (price)*. "Well, yes . . . here's what our economist thinks. . . . That's one way of looking at it, but you know . . . Okay . . . sure . . . good, okay . . . That's done. You sell 10 million at 98." While Shahri is closing the trade, a clerk has walked by several times dropping off tickets on her desk. She never looks at him, but he knows he has been acknowledged. She hangs up. Another line is blinking. It's an account who wants to get Shahri's view of the market—the duetsche mark has depreciated against the U.S. dollar. Shahri pulls up a foreign exchange chart on the monitor. Simultaneously a trader's voice comes across on the a loudspeaker: "Listen up. Tim just sold 35 million of World Bank. We've got 20 million left.

Let's try to move this paper today. Good work, Tim."
A low and less brash tone follows. It is the economist
giving his opinion of interest rates in the next six
months. Shahri, still on the phone, leans forward to
adjust the sound on the intercom. A minute passes.
Her call is done. She hangs up, sighs, jots down a note
in a spiral notebook. Without hesitation, she picks up
were she left off fifteen minutes earlier—true vestiges
of a salesperson. "Oh, that's the other thing I do—a
lot at once." The business of buying and selling securities might not have been what Shahri's parents, a
homemaker and an engineer, had in mind when they
told their four children to go out and make a difference in the world. But Shahri, thirty, has always
wanted to be in an career that gave her a view of
everything. And she says being an international bond
salesperson gives her a "global perspective." Later in
the day, after the market had closed, Shahri and I talk
over drinks. As we are seated, Shahri explains, "I have
always been curious about what exists beyond my
backyard. I think it has a lot to do with my childhood
experience overseas. " Born in Connecticut, Shahri
lived in the United States until age seven, when her
father's job relocated his family to Versailles, France.
Spending her formative years in a French public school
gave Shahri an appreciation for the cultures. She was
also influenced by her older sister, Cynthia, who studied languages. By the time she returned to the States,
at age twelve, she was not only extremely fluent in

French, she understood the importance of knowing the role other economies play in the world. "Quite often, as a people, we are concerned only with what's happening right around us. Most of us never really stop and notice that we are only a part of a much greater picture—I am very glad that I learned that earlier in life. What happens yesterday thousands of miles away may have a big impact on us today, if not tomorrow. That's why I am a strong supporter of our youth learning to speak more than their own language. It at the very least allows you to understand about other people."

As international experience relates to the professional career she chose, she continues, "I chose to be in international sales on Wall Street because it is the financial nerve center of the U.S. and to a great extent the rest of the world. The Street plays an enormous role in economies in nearly every region of the globe, whether we realize or not. For example, every large industrialized country has used debt or bond financings as a vehicle for funding its country's growth.

"As a international-debt salesperson, part of my job is to understand the financial as well as political environment in countries such as Canada, Germany, France, Britain, and Japan, among others. It's exciting because it's the only job where I really do have to know what's going on in the world. I enjoy having that type of knowledge."

Shahri graduated from the Wharton Business

School in 1990. At Wharton her concentration was finance. Shahri, a highly quantitative individual, majored in finance because, she says, "I have always worked well with numbers. Even in college, at Harvard, I liked knowing there was a definitive solution to every problem." Following Wharton, Shahri worked at two major investment houses. At one of the houses she says she was fortunate to have a woman mentor who taught her the ropes. However, she adds, "It's still tough being a woman and person of color in this industry. Fortunately, I had a well-respected senior woman mentor who taught me how to deal with the politics of being sometimes the only woman in a male environment. And that (politics) is a facet of business no matter what business or country you're working in. The best advice I can pass on to women, other than being open-minded about the way they view the world, is to realize that you must be resilient in every endeavor. There are many people who will say that because you are a woman you are not strong enough to handle tough decisions or that if you're a person of color, you might not have the skills to do the job. Regardless of those challenges to your desire and intelligence, stay steadfast and on task."

Carol Green

Shaping the Future

It was hard to accept, especially for this former runway model with a svelte physique. But it was true. One night while standing in front of a full-length mirror dressing for a black-tie affair, Carol Green saw in her reflection souvenirs from the birth of two children—a postpartum stomach which no exercise regime or strict weight loss program would erase. Far too fashionable for an outdated girdle but longing to fit into her slinky close-fitting Valentino dress, Carol pondered what to do and a light went off.

Necessity is truly the mother of invention. When Carol Green, CEO and president of Laracris Corporation, created a body-slimming shape wear known as Aubergine, French for eggplant (the same color of her logo, a deep purple bow), she answered the prayers of thousands of women and mothers, at the top of the list herself. This modern day pioneer entered the male-dominated innerwear industry in 1989. Her goal was to reinvent a foundation garment that would give all women firmer support while being a sophisticated compliment to their wardrobes. Enlisting the help of a pattern maker, Carol, a former model, made her designs, contracted a manufacturer, and sold the idea to buyers of some of the most well-known department stores in the country.

When Carol started out, however, there was some discouragement in the direction she took with marketing. "There were people who wanted to categorize my product as 'ethnic,' " recalls Carol on a call from her Chicago-based office. "Some thought because I am an African-American woman that my product was geared only to women of color. I told them black women weren't the only women who wear foundations or have weight problems.

"Although I believe ethnic products are wonderful, I didn't want to market Aubergine as a 'for ethnic people only' product because I knew that it would limit the sales to only one market," explains Carol, who says the first retail buyers of Aubergine was Marshall Fields, a major department store in Chicago. "However, we do have a line, Complexion Perfection, whose colors are suited for the many skin tones of women of color. But in general, I wanted people to know Aubergine is for everybody. I know there are many women who have run into the same kind of problems when marketing their products which have a broader market appeal. One piece of advice I'd give is to take your product to as many people who will buy it. I have always felt if you have a good product don't limit yourself." Fortunately Carol knew Aubergine had "mass appeal," and the tenaciousness to market and sell as such paid off. The popular line of shapewear has not only been highlighted in *Essence* magazine, but also in *Vogue, Glamour, Haper's Bazaar* and *Self.* It's no wonder that with a wider market, Laracris Corporation has nearly tripled in size since its inception. Now Carol's Lycra creations comes in three lines to be exact: Aubergine, Aubergine Too and Complexion Perfection. The collection of midriff tops, half slips, camisoles, unitards, and bodysuits are being worn by women everywhere—even by some of the most recognized names in the entertainment industry. "My shapewear is special because it is the only high-quality inner wear that comfortably firms, shapes, and is beautiful. I'll admit, though, I did have those start-up jitters over whether it would catch on." But after Aubergine hit the market, there wasn't a problem with people catching on. In fact, her shapewear became so successful she had to create a mail order catalog, *Inner Circle,* when thousands of customers called her in frustration after learning their favorite Aubergine styles had been sold out in exclusive clothing stores such as Neiman-Marcus, Nordstroms, and Bergdorf Goodman. Even though widespread success of Aubergine (which is also sold in Japan and Canada) came from not allowing others to limit how she sells her shapewear, Carol says that didn't stop her from having the same problems that many women and people of color have when starting their businesses. "Obtaining a line

of credit was one of the biggest challenges," cites
Carol, whose husband, radiologist Dr. Richard Green
gave her the initial start-up capital. "I am very lucky
to have had support. But I know that's not the case
for most of us. Most people don't understand how
difficult it is to start a business without a business loan
or a line of credit. For example, it even took a line of
credit to purchase the fabric for the prototypes.

"That's why I often tell women who asked me
about starting businesses to make sure you do the research and know what it takes for them to get their
products to the market."

Born in Port Arthur, Texas, Carol attended college
at Southwestern University, where she majored in
business. Before Carol started her company, she mod-
eled professionally, during which time she met and
married her husband. She left modeling to become a
mother and gave birth to two children—Lauren and
Christian—after whom her company, Laracris Inc., is
named. Although Laracris keeps Carol on the road,
she says her family ranks above everything else. Her
extra time is spent working out and volunteering with
her favorite charities—Bryant Ballet, a foundation that
teaches inner-city children classical ballet, and the
McDermott Foundation, an organization that assists
homeless, drug and alcohol addicts—and educating
her children through world travels to places like
Monte Carlo, London, and Paris.

Lisa Cowan

Young and Talented

On a proud and ceremonious day in May of 1993, the illustrious Oprah Winfrey addresses an audience of 407 "Queens"—the graduating class of Spelman College. Their faces glisten with tears as they listen to Oprah's memorable message, filled with personal, uplifting, and valuable lessons that will be permanently etched on their minds as they take on life outside of academia. Side by side the Queens of Spelman College savor the monumental words of wisdom from the talk show Queen.

W HEN LISA COWAN GRADUATED FROM SPELMAN College, she walked away with more than the ability to take her sociology degree and turn it into a career in finance. Lisa was one of nine graduating seniors in her class to land a job on Wall Street. However, the twenty-two-year-old New York native says she also took from her four years at the historically all-women's college, "the inner strength to overcome obstacles"—many of which she faced well outside of her sisterly campus in Atlanta, Georgia, soon after graduation. Regardless of what lay ahead, Lisa knew, as she had heard from Oprah, "A queen is not afraid to live, nor is she afraid to fail. . . . Failure is the stepping stone to greatness." And Lisa had to learn to walk through life's difficult situations "like a queen."

From the table of an open roof restaurant, Lisa Cowan, now twenty-four, stares out mystically at the faces that pass by. A subtle smile suggests a pleasant disposition, but it's clear something rests deeper in her conversation. She neatly unfolds her napkin and places it in her lap. At the beginning she explains that she is in the process of making a career change. Lisa was planning to leave her Wall Street job as a bond broker. "I felt very limited because the position did not fulfill my expectations. And after two years, I decided I needed to move."

It's not uncommon for most people to change jobs to enhance career development and for better opportunities. In fact, on average most people change jobs six times in their career. And like most people starting in professional careers, Lisa's decision to change for greater experiences was a wise one. But Lisa goes beyond the usual "better opportunity" explanation to detail the underpinnings of her decision. She says, "It's unrealistic to assume that throughout your career you won't have a job that doesn't meet your expectations from a career development and advancement perspective. Of course, the experience of deciding how to handle the situation can knock you around a bit, as it did me. But the real maturity—the ability to walk through it 'like a queen'—is how gracefully you handle your exit and the choices you make in your next career." When Lisa departed from the financial company, she left on good terms and also knowing that she wanted more from her next employer. "I want to be in a position that gives me a broader base of skills and exposure. I plan on going to business school soon, and I want a career that prepares me for it. "

Several months after our initial meeting, I speak to Lisa again. She works as an analyst for Deloitte & Touche Consulting Group. At Deloitte & Touche, Lisa is in a training program where she was assigned to a variety of management consulting engagements in the public and financial sectors. "There's no doubt it was definitely a good decision. But above being a good career decision, I feel I learned a lot about myself as a person and as a businessperson. The best advice that I can give women at my stage in their careers is to be honest with themselves about what it is they want in the long term; if not long term, intermediate term. And most of all, don't be afraid to admit to yourself that it's time to move on."

Teresa Clarke

Golden Opportunities

There are only a few people who consistently find golden career opportunities. Teresa Clarke is one of those people. For most of Teresa's professional life it seems as if everything fell into place. Starting as early as her time at Harvard University, Teresa was a "perennial summer intern" who landed jobs with top investment houses and banks in New York, Paris, and Brazil. After she completed Harvard's prestigious joint MBA and JD program in 1989, she landed an enviable position inside the real estate department at a major investment firm where she advanced to become a vice president. But after hitting the "glass ceiling" in 1994, the thirty-three-year-old investment banker spent some time figuring out the answer to the infamous question: "What next?" This was the first time she found herself at a crossroad. And that caused Teresa to step back and reassess herself and what she valued the most. Fortunately for Teresa she did and her next career opportunity was truly "golden."

BEFORE TERESA DEPARTS TO SOUTH AFRICA IN November of 1995 to take on new career opportunities which had developed for her, we spend a couple hours over dinner discussing why she has decided to move

to a land which, only a year and a half earlier in April
of 1994, had gone through a monumental change after
the free elections that made Nelson Mandela president
of South Africa. Teresa, a medium-frame woman
whose flawless complexion shows no signs of someone
accustomed to the stress of working eighty-plus hour
weeks, described how she reached her decision. "In
making the career move, I sought to achieve more than
professional recognition and attractive financial re-
muneration. I have always spent a significant portion
of my free time working with community organizations. Like many black people, I came from a family
with a long history of professional involvement in social services; my mother was a teacher and is now a
superintendent of schools. My grandmother managed
three federally funded child care centers for low-
income families. They have both been wonderful role
models for me as well as examples of career women
who have made it to the top of their respective fields
while making significant contributions toward the betterment of their communities. Despite my love for finance, I have always felt an internal desire to
contribute to the betterment of the world from a social
perspective. South Africa provided an unparalled opportunity to 'do well' while 'doing good.' When I first
visited South Africa as a tourist earlier this year, the
black people in the country made me feel so wel-
comed. When they inquired about my profession, they

looked me in the eye and strongly encouraged me to return to their country. 'We need black people with your skills' is what they told me. For the first time in my life, I felt that my skills were appreciated because I was black, not in spite of being black, as had always been the case in the U.S. South Africa after the free elections is like the U.S. in the postwar environment. There are so many opportunities surrounding you, the hardest challenge is prioritizing and choosing which golden opportunities to pursue."

Embracing a change such as picking up and relocating to South Africa, which Teresa had decided on doing before she even knew what opportunities awaited her, was a bold and courageous leap. And Teresa, in many ways like South Africa, truly couldn't have been more in the midst of a "liminal moment," to borrow the term from writer Shery Turkel. It means when things are betwixt and between, when old structures have broken down and new ones have not yet been created. Teresa agreed in saying, "It's an old adage, but change does create opportunity. Such was the case with both my careers and South Africa. Change in both ways made way for exciting new prospects. I think that things happen for a reason, and it is important to ask yourself why something good or bad has happened and ask, 'What can I learn from this?' "

Not long after Teresa arrived in her newfound home, I received a letter from her. The letter was printed on red stationery that was as rich and as bright as her new opportunity in a world well outside the fray on Wall Street.

DECEMBER 1995

Happy Holiday from South Africa:

I want to take this opportunity to share a little more than a basic "Happy Holiday."

I moved to Johannesburg in the fall and have been on a magic carpet ride since the day I set foot on the ground here. Things are going exceptionally well. This experience thus far has been exhilarating from professional, intellectual, social, and personal perspectives. There's so much optimism among the people. This truly is the "New" South Africa and it is amazing to witness the rebirth of a nation. What's so astounding is how quickly people have changed their attitudes about so many things which were so deeply entrenched in their socio-cultural underpinnings. There still is a long way to go on many fronts, but there is a sense of shared commitment on the whites and blacks to achieve their goals. I will start teaching at the University of Witwatersrand Graduate Business School (Wit is pronounced "Vits" for short) in late January. I will teach three courses next year: a basic finance course for graduate students in the one-year (mini-MBA) program, team-teach basic corporate finance in the MBA program with the head of the finance department; and teach my own advanced finance course which is an elective in the MBA program. I am very excited about joining the university and have found the faculty very welcoming. I have been asked to join the dean of the business school and a small delegation on a study tour of Hong Kong, Beijing, Bombay, and Delhi in January. The purpose of the trip is to examine the means of production and labor productivity in other emerging markets and learn what lessons can be useful to South Africa.

I am also involved in a number of private sector business activities. I have been consulting for Abt Associates, which is a public policy think tank headquartered in Cambridge, Mass. I have also become involved with a number of private equity transactions including two in the affordable housing development area.

I am very happy here and excited about the future of South Africa. There are wonderful opportunities here to help shape a new nation and participate in the plethora of change whether it is in business, education, health care, law, or just about any element of a society. Please feel free to visit or be in touch if you have any interest in

becoming involved in the change from a business
or professional standpoint.

Fondly,
Teresa

Since speaking with Teresa, she has become the Director of Abt Associates in South Africa and a partner in
KMM Investments, which has made several major ac-
quisitions in a variety of industries in South Africa. In
addition, she continues to teach part-time at the university.

Gloria Turner

The Risk Taker

It's clear that Gloria Turner has learned from listening to her gut feeling—that inner voice that tells her to seize hold of opportunities. "You don't get anywhere by always playing safe," remarks Gloria. "You have to be willing to make a stretch, take on the difficult challenges. If you don't, how will you ever know what you're capable of?"

GLORIA KNOWS ALL ABOUT TAKING RISK. IN THE early eighties she left her job in the quality-control laboratory at Philip Morris to return to college. Many pondered why? After all, Gloria had advanced to a respectable post in management with a two-year associate degree from John Tyler Community College and two years of pre-nursing from Bennett College, in Greensboro, North Carolina. Gloria wasn't satisfied, though, with just being a manager; she wanted to go further and knew that meant a four-year degree. At thirty-five she enrolled in Cornell University, and at thirty-seven she graduated with the backpack-toting students in Ithaca, New York. The thought of being singled out as a older student didn't bother Gloria; the reward was what she kept on her mind. Having the will to continue came from her large Southern family with nine uncles and three aunts who stressed education as the key to success. Listening to her elders paid off.

Today, Gloria Turner is a vice president at J. P. Morgan. At J. P. Morgan she is a grant maker, responsible for a budget of approximately $2 million, which is used to aid health, housing, community revitalization, and economic development in New York City. In addition, she facilitates corporate funding for employment training for adults as well as serves on numerous nonprofit advisory committees throughout the New York boroughs.

Gloria arrives at our Saturday afternoon lunch dressed casually wearing a Howard University cap and a small African medallion. This youthful fifty-year-old Virginian woman explained how she got to J. P. Morgan from Cornell University and how showing chutzpah has helped in her career. "At Cornell University you had two ways of obtaining positions upon graduation. You could bid points or submit your résumé for pre-screening when corporations came on campus to recruit. I submitted my résumé for prescreening. When J. P. Morgan selected my résumé in the prescreening process, I thought someone had made a mistake. I say that because my background was in prenursing, plus I had worked for fifteen years managing quality control laboratories at Firestone and

Phillip Morris before returning to finish my undergraduate degree. I spoke to an officer in the career
placement office, and he said, 'Are you crazy? People
kill for these types of opportunities. Go on the interview!' I did my research and decided on the area I
wanted to be placed. It turned out the recruiter had
not made a mistake and was actually looking for candidates with my skill set. He assured me I wasn't in
the wrong place and after the initial interview invited
me to their New York office for more rounds. The
interviews went quite well, and they offered me a position in the operations management training program." After Gloria started with J. P. Morgan's
operations management program, she found a mentor
at the firm to help guide and shape her development.
"Mentors are critical in any business," she continues,
"because you don't know what's going on starting
out. I'd even say they are the difference in many cases
between success and failure. For example, I came in
the program with a group of forty or fifty other train-
ees. Out of that group, a senior vice president selected
six individuals whom he would give special assignments to. I was one of those six. I didn't realize it at
the time, but he was my first mentor at the firm. We
had informal sessions and meetings to discuss the
events of the week. He'd solicit my opinion, give me
feedback and specific tasks where he'd later follow up
with his senior officers to learn how I handled those
assignments. I think being privy to that kind of guid-

ance early on in my career played a substantial role in
my development over the years." While internal support played a huge part of her career, Gloria credits
her willingness to take on the more difficult assignments in her field. "I've been with the company for
almost fourteen years, and I've worked in different areas over that time." She continues, "I'd say the
greatest challenge of my career was the cash management sales position. I say this for two reasons. First,
young people going into business careers need to understand that *you have to be a risk taker*. Second, *you
have to be willing to go the distance*. When I inter-
viewed for the cash management position, I literally
did not have time to prepare. The head of the cash
management division flew in from Brussels the afternoon I found out about the job. They called me the
next morning and said, 'The manager is in town, can
you come in to meet him at nine?' I said *YES!* I didn't
even know the definition of cash management, but I
knew I couldn't say no. I said to myself, 'I am going
in. If he ask me questions I can't answer, I'll tell him
the situation, I'll be honest, but I want this great opportunity!' In the interview he asked me very general
questions related to sales and management. I was positive and enthusiastic. I answered all his questions confidently, and I got the job! When I got into the
position, I didn't know anything about the products,"
she recalled with a slight smile. "It was extremely hard
for me because I worked with many people who had

far more years of experience. At first, I did feel as if I was looked upon as such a junior person. In order to get over the insecurity, I stayed many late nights and taught myself the products, in addition to the training that I was receiving from the company. I also read everything from *Newsweek* to *Business Week*. Whatever my clients were reading, I was reading it, too. I spent time teaching myself until I started to speak to them with confidence. Socially, I became very knowledgeable about wines, which helped me in informal settings such as dinners. It takes time to become knowledgable in a new setting or business. So, I'd say you have to be willing to make a stretch. It may mean getting someone's help or enlisting other guidance, but you can't be afraid to do it. *Take the risk!*"

MBA—Must Be Aggressive

By six o'clock an empty auditorium starts to fill up. MBAs from one of the nation's most prestigious graduate programs are seated side by side for a corporate information session. Forty or more outwardly tenacious candidates pay close attention to corporate representatives (potential employers)— being careful not to miss names or points of discussion. This is one of few chances to make introductions and good impressions.

LIKE THE THOUSANDS OF BUSINESSPEOPLE IN THE country, Grace Vandecruze has a Masters in Business Administration (MBA). The two-year graduate business degree has become a highly sought after credential, particularly among African-Americans. In 1992 alone nearly 4,000 African-American men and women were awarded MBAs. And each year the National Black MBA Association hosts a conference which draws thousands of up-and-coming African-American professionals. With so many more African-Americans earning professional degrees, it may seem that all it takes is having an MBA to land a job with a major corporation. Not the thinking with Grace. The thirty-

two-year-old Wharton MBA graduate adamantly expresses that having an MBA, even from a top school
such as Wharton, definitely has its advantages, but it
doesn't mean that finding a permanent position or a
summer internship is automatic. The bottom line is—
you have to be aggressive in marketing your credentials.

On a Sunday, inside her Upper West Side apartment, Grace, an associate in the corporate finance department at Merrill Lynch, clears away plates from
brunch and the misconception about MBAs. "It was
not so much my degree as it was the *degree* to which
I had to work for the right career opportunity," comments Grace in an easy-spirited Caribbean-influenced
accent. Grace, a Guyanese native, says in a melodious
voice, "Sometimes we have to choose schools we
know the companies are going to recruit from. We
know by going to those schools that we'll stand a better chance of finding a job, but it's no guarantee." In
an account Grace describes how her own experience
with finding a position was an indication that even
with an MBA from a top school, you still have to
work hard to get positions inside major companies.

"When I was looking for a summer position between my first and second year in business school, I
submitted my résumé to the placement center at Wharton, but my résumé was not selected by any of the
companies I was interested in. Subsequently I had to
seek out the key people at the firms and make an in-

troduction. I went through a number of brochures, found names, and made calls. In making calls I asked for informal meetings which gave me the chance to visit their company. That was key because no one will take the time to find out who you are so you must put yourself in front of them and say, 'I'm qualified and this is what I can do.' "

Before Grace graduated from the Wharton MBA program in 1993, she worked for three and a half years at Ernst & Young, a major accounting firm. To further distinguish herself, she took and passed the certified public accountant exam (CPA). In addition, Grace has a bachelor's degree in accounting from Pace University. In spite of her strong "quantitative background," which is highly regarded among professionals in her field, Grace made the point: "When you're competing in a field where most people have gone to the top programs in the country, you have to assume that everyone has a 'strong background.' What sets you apart from the person who is also a CPA and worked for an accounting firm, or the person who may just have more inroads or contacts, is how much harder you sell yourself, especially when the opportunity doesn't come to you."

Networking with other African-American men and women, Grace says, was extremely helpful in exposing her to the key people inside her company, but it wasn't the only factor in getting her foot in the door. Grace goes on to explain that casting a wider net was very important to her success. "Clearly, we have come a long way in our sense of commitment to each other. By this, I mean networking with one another has served us well as far as getting chances that we might not have ever had. But in most cases, the decision makers are not African-American people. Therefore, it's stifling to think, 'I'm only going to meet with the black guy in this department or the black woman in this office.' You really have to be broader in thinking about who can help you accomplish your goals." Grace did accomplish her goals; she was hired as a summer associate. After the summer Grace accepted a permanent offer to return after graduation.

Now, after four years at Merrill Lynch, Grace has become a recognized team member in the company's corporate finance department. "Being aggressive doesn't just stop with getting inside. I am more aggressive when it comes to my performance at work and making sure that I'm viewed as an exemplary member of my team," she says. Grace participates on a number of mergers and acquisition deals for financial institutions. Her position entails performing the research and analytical evaluations necessary to properly advise her company's clients on the best methods to attain financing in the equity and debt markets. Grace's style may best be summarized by Lee Whitely, an African-American male associate and colleague in her department: "I think Grace has a great ability to make sure people know she is competent without seeming overbearing or self-serving. And that goes a long way because being aggressive doesn't mean anything if it is not handled with some finesse or *grace*."

Angela Brock-Kyle

Two Degrees of Success

Angela Brock Kyle, associate director in the Private Placement* Division at Teacher's Insurance Annuity Association/College Retirement Equity Fund, (TIAA/CREF), knows that it takes more than just a professional degree to get inside the top positions. "Sometimes, it takes two," she says. And though Angela, a business and law school graduate, says dual degrees are less common with rising educational costs, she still firmly believes the more credentials that women of color have, the better their chances are for advancing in the corporate world.

At the nation's largest private pension fund, Angela is surrounded by cherrywood furniture in her windowed office while she speaks about degrees, measuring success, and what has elevated her career. "I felt having two degrees would make me more marketable while giving me extra skills to draw upon. I don't think you need to have an MBA and JD to get

---

Private placement is the direct sale of stocks or bonds by an issuer to an institutional investor.

a job in a corporation. But I do feel that in many instances you need to have at least an MBA to advance.
Based on my experiences and the experiences of others, I have learned that the more tools you have in
your arsenal the better. As women of color, it be-
hooves us to have the credentials to surmount the hurdles." Before Angela completed the MBA/JD program
from UCLA in 1984, she earned a finance and marketing degree from Cal State University in Hayward,
California. Angela focused on business at the advice
of her father, a professional man. He felt that he had
not advanced in his career as far as his intelligence
warranted in part because he did not pursue a graduate education. He did not want his daughter to have
the same limitations. But even with two professional
degrees, Angela states "the hurdles" still exist. While
in graduate school at UCLA, Angela noticed that other
African-American students were having problems finding employment after graduation. Determined that she
would not be in the same predicament, Angela took a
nontraditional route to securing her position. "I said
to myself, 'I'm going to have to use more resources
than the career placement office to make sure I obtain
suitable employment,' " Angela wrote directly to the
chief financial officer (CFO) of the companies she
wanted to work for. One of her inquiries for a position
was answered by the CFO of RCA, who hired her
within twenty-four hours. She worked directly for the
CFO for two years as a financial associate. Although

corresponding with the CFO of a company was not standard practice, Angela expressed that her direct contact strategy was based on the belief that "if the functional area you want to work wants to hire you, they can pass that information on to human resources and make it happen. In addition, fundamentally, I believe that we as African-American people simply have to *push harder*." Pushing harder has propelled Angela into the officer ranks within her department. Another factor to her success is knowing how to leverage off of her professional attributes, she explains. "I think you have to be able to honestly access your strengths and weaknesses. Transform your weaknesses into strengths and play to those strengths. Make sure that others recognize and reward your performance. Enable others to help your career by requesting feedback, developing mentors, modifying your career strategy when appropriate, and pursuing your plans with single-minded determination. Always make it easy for your colleagues to support you and enhance your success."

And though this thirty-something loan officer can look at the two mounted degrees as well as cite a string of aggressive decisions she has made in her position at TIAA as proof of her success, she doesn't. The biggest reminder, at work, that she is doing well comes from her jovial doe-eyed toddler, Brock, who smiles back at her from a photo on her desk. A married working mother, Angela says, "Of course it is a challenge to be a wife and working mother, but it is possible. I do believe that we can have both (career and a family). However, it takes work and you have to know what it is you want. The key to effectively balancing a family and a career is being good to yourself. Too many women sacrifice their health and peace of mind to ensure that their families are comfortable and satisfied. These women are the foundation for a smooth-running household and office. Do what you need to do to keep yourself as relaxed, healthy, and happy as you can. Do that half-day spa thing, take an hour for a bubble bath, read a novel, just be good to yourself. If you're not good to yourself, you can't expect others to be good to you, and if you're worn and frazzled, you can't give your best to all those people who rely on you. Undeniably, you want to be recognized and rewarded for your efforts and commitment in your career. Equally, you also want the flexibility to spend with your family and raise your children." In the investment world Angela works on what is known as the *buy side*—hedge, mutual, money, and pension fund managers. There is less of a time demand on the buy side. Angela's days in the office can be long, but for the most part, she says, "it in no way compares to the hours of those on the sell side"—investment bankers and other securities professionals—which she says makes her life more manageable. "This side of the investment business is more family friendly, which I recognized when looking for a position. I strongly recommend that women select a career in business fields that allow them to balance family and career demands. It is as much of a challenge to be a good wife and good parent as it is to excel your career. Finding a career that did not sacrifice one for the other was paramount." But Angela notes, "Now, I don't take all the credit for doing everything. I do have help," she says, referring to her husband, the owner of a sales and marketing outsource company.

Since seventy percent of all African-American families are headed by women, Angela says she does feel fortunate "to have a husband who supports me in my career and with the raising of our child. Which brings me to what it takes to find a quality mate in life," she says with a smile in a near testimonial. "I think many women with professional aspirations have to invest significant time and effort in the pursuit of a career. Unfortunately, they don't take the same time and approach to selecting a mate. Some women must be flexible enough to consider men with unrecognized potential. Money and looks can come and go; it's the essence of the man that will remain with you. Too many women settle for men with the right 'credentials' who don't give them the respect and admiration they deserve. Once you know who you are and what characteristics you truly need in a mate, then make a plan to find your man." And that's exactly what Angela

did. Happily married, she says, "We both work hard
to have as strong a family life as we do successful careers. And because of this, I definitely feel there are
really two scales by which I, like most women, measure my success."

Lisa Caesar

Trading Up

There are about 8,000 miles between the United States and Hong Kong, and Lisa Caesar travels them all several times a year. For some, the idea of making routine twelve-hour trips to the Far East on business may seem a bit daunting, but it's all a part of the job for Lisa Caesar—executive director in the Fixed Income Department at Peregrine Incorporated, an Asian investment bank based in Hong Kong. Peregrine markets and distributes Asian debt securities. At Peregrine, Lisa oversees all debt sales activity for the company's New York office.

PARK SLOPE, BROOKLYN, IS ABOUT AS FAR AWAY AS Lisa Caesar can be from the glittering skyline of Hong Kong, a city of 6.3 million people and the eighth-largest trading economy in the world. And for the time being, that is good for the busy executive. In fact, for the next hour there's no discussion on how the world will view Hong Kong post June 30, 1997—when the British crown returns Hong Kong to China nor how sales orders for Asian debt securities will be affected by the political changing of the guard. The order of the day is cappuccino. And I am speaking with Lisa shortly before she departs to the Pacific Rim for three months. Our discussion is on how she's handling life as one of the most senior African-American women in her field. Lisa is at ease in her neighborhood coffee shop, sitting on the barstool comfortably dressed with her hair pushed away from her face, which makes one think she is a local college student. But the thirty-four-year-old Milwaukee-raised executive's style is anything but staid or sophomoric when it comes to running multimillion-dollar transactions and putting her company on the map. As the executive director of sales at Peregrine, Lisa spends much of her time educating American investors on Asian debt securities and overseeing the sales division of thirty-plus professionals. Since Lisa took over her current position in 1994, she says taking on the position of executive director of sales "has been the biggest challenge of my career yet." The Harvard MBA, who was a commercial paper trader for six years at Lehman Brothers before moving to Peregrine, explained what it has taken for her to run an international debt operation. "One of the first adjustments I had to make going from domestic to foreign was understanding the vast differences which exist between the markets in the U.S. At Lehman, I traded money-market instruments, which are primarily short-term debt securities such as: certificates of deposits (CDs) and banker's acceptances. Being that the short-term sector of the U.S. debt market is the most liquid or efficient sector in the financial markets, it was a dramatic shift to move into a foreign market, where the markets are not as liquid and have emerged only in the past decade. But what is exciting in this arena is there is so much growth which translates into business for a company such as ours." Another adjustment Lisa had to make for her career change was the cultural differences of the people with whom she works. "Peregrine employs approximately a thousand people and it's very diverse. In my office, I am maybe one of a handful of Americans, forget being black or a woman. Working in this environment makes you appreciate more how we all can be different but have the same objectives." But market and cultural differences weren't the only changes that Lisa had to make. "It does require numerous trips. Which means I'm away from home," says Lisa, who praises the support of her husband, Francis, an attorney.

Learning how to marshal resources to bring her department together was also a big challenge for her. In the beginning Lisa spent seventeen-hour days building the Peregrine Fixed Income Division. She recalled her first day of walking on the debt sales floor. "There wasn't a fixed income department," she recounts comically. "There wasn't a department—no phones, desks, employees, nothing. Part of my initial responsibility was to establish the fixed income operation in the New York office. It was completely entrepreneurial in one respect. It took a lot of work to get the office up and

running." With the help of her managers and coun-
terparts in Hong Kong, Lisa explained, she was able
to successfully organize the department and bring in
deals. "The department has come a long way from
that first day," she says somewhat reflective.

After Lisa graduated from Oberlin College in
1984, she landed a job with Morgan Stanley working
in the Management and Information Systems Department. Lisa's job was technical support, which required
her to be a liaison between the data systems department and the traders in the front office. Working directly with the traders, Lisa recalled, "sparked my
interest more than my internships in banking. What
appealed to me was the incredible amount of responsibility a young trader can have early in his or her
career. It is also very transaction- and team-oriented,
which makes the job very exciting." Not long after
working at Lehman, Lisa quickly established herself.
"Having a lot of responsibility gave me the chance to
prove my abilities," she says. And Lisa's abilities
played a huge part in her landing and maintaining a
job in trading. She admits to also "being charmed."
"I was fortunate in that my managers demonstrated
an interest in my development. One manager told me,
'Lisa, I want you to do well, and, genuinely mean it.'
That confidence made a big difference in my career
and the type of impression I left while I worked there."
And maybe the greatest proof of how much of an im-

pression Lisa made came in 1993. When a few of her colleagues left Lehman to work as senior managers for Peregrine, they presented Lisa with the opportunity to join them as Executive Director of debt sales.

Cristal Baron

Putting in the Time

At half-past midnight a fifteen-hour day comes to an end for Cristal Baron. With briefcase in hand, the thin-framed woman walks through the marbled floor galleria of the World Financial Center, pushes the revolving doors, and steps onto a scarcely populated sidewalk. While flagging the car service outside the office building, she thinks about the day—her mind searches for any forgotten tasks. The numbered car pulls up. As Cristal closes the door, she takes solace in knowing her work is done, at least the part that can be completed for the day. The black town car drives off, and soon the West Side Manhattan skyline grows to full view from the rear window. Cristal peers out from her private carriage as it makes its way across the Brooklyn Bridge. In a few hours it starts all over again.

THE LONG-AWAITED QUIET AND SOLITUDE COMES AS Cristal turns the key, opens the door, and hits the light switch. Inside her high-ceilinged loft apartment Cristal checks her messages and flips through mail. After a few minutes she is relaxed on a sofa in her living room. "This is *my* time," she remarks with a smile while reading a letter from one of her Delta Sigma

Theta Sorority sisters from her home in Washington. Finding time even to read letters comes at a premium for this twenty-seven-year-old banker in the Municipal Capital Markets Division at Merrill Lynch. Often her days of financial modeling and preparation can end well past midnight. And on the night we speak, 12:30 A.M., she says it is an "early evening." Nonetheless, Cristal, accustomed to long workdays, accepts the schedule of her life for now. She expresses, "In order to be where you want to be, you have to be willing to put in the time. If anything is worthwhile, it is worth a sacrifice. I'd imagine for most younger people, starting out, it is difficult to give up a great deal of personal time—parties, social gatherings—for a career but it can sometimes be a necessary evil to see results." For Cristal, the long-term results equal more responsibility and involvement in her department.

Cristal learned the value of postponing immediate gratification for long-term reward long before her days as a career woman. It was something her mother, an administrator at Howard University, taught her. "My mother always told me you have to be twice as good to get anywhere in this world, and oftentimes that means working twice as hard." While Cristal attended Howard University, where she majored in journalism and minored in business, she spent most of her extra time gaining experience in the news business. She worked part-time for Howard University's newspaper, the *Hilltop*, and its television station, WHMM Channel 32. The reward of youthful tenacity paid off in her last year. "During my senior year I landed a plum internship with ABC's *Nightline* with Ted Koppel. Working in what is considered the height of broadcast journalism gave me an appreciation for what I had achieved and also the time I had spent getting there."

Cristal's persistent path did not end there. A week after she graduated from Howard, she began working as a financial reporter with Dow Jones News Services in Washington, where she was responsible for covering the Federal Reserve Board, the U.S. Treasury, State and Labor Departments, and the U.S. Congress among other things. "I covered places such as the World Bank and the African Development Bank and in doing so developed an interest in infrastructure finance in developing countries." Deciding that she would change paths, Cristal went to McGill University, in Montreal, Canada. "Many of the graduates from the program go on to work in fields that promote community and economic development in underdeveloped countries, through the public and private sectors." However, at McGill, Cristal realized, two years of business school training would not adequately prepare her for the types of opportunities she wanted to pursue. To improve her understanding of infrastructure finance and enhance her credentials, Cristal turned to Wall Street, specifically looking at public finance. What really attracted Cristal to public finance was the ability of the public finance bankers to assist state and local govern-

mental agencies and their authorities in raising capital
to finance highways, airports, hospitals, public power,
and other public projects. Though public finance has
not provided her with the international focus she
sought in pursuing business school, she believes it has
rewarded her with stronger credentials and constant
challenges. "One of the aspects that I most enjoy in
my position is the ability to develop financially creative solutions to our client needs," she says. "Creativ-
ity has manifested itself in many ways in my various
career pursuits. It is important to me. It keeps me from
getting bored."

Bithiah Carter

Changing Perceptions

It's 6:30 A.M.—A subway platform is full of people waiting for a Manhattan-bound train, which has been delayed by a water main break two stations away. Bithiah Carter, thirty-one, stands at the edge of the platform, leans forward, and looks for the two headlights that should have appeared in the dark tunnel fifteen minutes ago. A few minutes pass and the train pulls into the station. A frustrated mob pushes its way into the double doors and pensively waits for the conductor's admonition to "Step in. Stand clear of the door." Compressed back to back with other commuters, the young businesswoman holds on tightly to the strap hanger for the next six stops into Manhattan while reading a quarter-folded paper. She has a few minutes to find out what didn't make news on Bloomberg, a financial news retrieval service.

D AY AFTER DAY, FOR EIGHT YEARS, THIS HAS BEEN the morning ritual for Bithiah Carter, thirty-one, salesperson at W. R. Lazard, a minority-owned investment bank based in New York. For many career women, the motivation to be in highly competitive careers such as sales—careers that require a large degree of persistence—is to be paid well and recognized in their profession. However, for some women, there are other reasons. Bithiah Carter, an energetic and attractive woman, has another reason, which she shares with me at her home in Brooklyn. Inside a modestly decorated apartment, Bithiah explains over a glass of wine that one of the other reasons she is motivated to be in her career is to change perceptions. The Cleveland State graduate from Ohio stated, "I am pushed to be in a business career first and foremost because of the knowledge I acquire. That may sound a little clichéd, but that really is my reason." Bithiah explains further, "Like anyone who works, of course there are the basic needs that we must meet. Those needs drive us to get up each morning and go in. But whatever underlying reason we chose certain areas versus others has more to do with the way we see ourselves and the way in which we want others to see us. For example, it amazes me that some of us have limited views on what we can do in the business world. There have been a number of times where others are shocked when I tell them what I do for a living. That tells me a lot about how we, specifically, as African-Americans, still today, perceive what we are capable of doing. And I'll admit, sometimes it bothers me." But Bithiah is not trying to alter everyone's perception of what she is capable of doing professionally. "No, I don't try to change the perception of every person I meet. However, I do hope I am making a difference with the younger people—the children," she says. As a visiting mentor to a class of third graders at a local elementary school in her community, she says, "That's where I hope to change the mindset. It's exciting to watch the faces of children brighten with interest when they learn I am doing something that is different from what they have been taught or exposed to. It piques their curiosity and makes them want to learn more. Of course, I don't expect all of them to want to grow up and become brokers or salespeople. But I do hope their expectations of what they are capable of accomplishing, in spite of everything around them, has been changed."

"Also," she says, switching to a lighter tone, "I am motivated to be in this business because I want to know everything."

"Call me nosey! I've always been the kind of person who wanted to know what's happening in the world, the business world. Why did this company sell its interest in this company? Or why will one company decide to move its headquarters to another country and what will that mean for people with jobs at that company?

"I don't care whether you're buying toothpaste or a new car. Every dollar you spend translates at some point in time to a buy or sell for investors. And that drives business. Realizing all of this is at the heart of what drives me to be a business professional.

"Often someone will ask me how do I handle working in a environment made up of mostly white males or do I feel I can really get ahead when there are so few black women in senior positions? I always find those questions interesting, but my answer is usually simple. I tell them, 'How does this environment differ from many other places in America or corporate America?' How about finding success? Success?" she says, thinking deeply about the definition. "Well, for the first time in history, we are reaching heights that we have never reached before. No longer are we only in the back offices, but some of us have moved into the boardrooms. You see us at some of the top levels in corporations and even running our own businesses. But that doesn't define how successful we have become as professional black women. I think our success is better defined by how we take what we have gained from our experiences, personally and professionally, and use it to advance our presence in the next century. In my mind, that's making sure the generation to follow can benefit from our success and mistakes."

Brenda Neal

Staying Power

She appeared on the pages of *Essence* magazine like an icon—dressed in a classic black suit with a hand-tailored collar. She stands with her hands clasped, exuding trust and confidence. In 1989 *Essence* magazine featured Brenda Neal as one of the African-American career women at the top. Brenda, then forty-five, worked for the junk bond powerhouse—Drexel Burnham Lambert, now defunct. Although Drexel is no longer around, Brenda is. The sixteen-year investments veteran credits her staying power to being a market-smart professional and strong believer that being a knowledgeable communicator is one of the keys to succcss.

Brenda Neal is a financial consultant at Smith Barney in New York. In her business she directs and works with investment assets for an account base of institutions and individual investors with concentrations in the stock and bond markets. She also conducts investment seminars for businesses and individuals who are unfamiliar with the process of investing. Twenty years ago most people would have called Brenda a stockbroker because that was the only name to describe the people who took market orders and maintained the agent relationship between brokerage firms and the general public. That has changed dramatically—the industry has become more complex in terms of type of financial products available to the investing public. Securities sales professionals, who are called upon to know more about the products they sell, go by names like account executives, financial consultants, financial advisers, and so forth. With all the fuss over names it is hard to know the difference between account executive and financial consultant. I visit with Brenda, fifty-three, at work to find out what was really in a name. Inside her office the walls are ornamented by achievement plaques and awards, and it's immediately clear that there's a lot in the name, especially when it comes to Brenda. Her name is inscribed under the words TOP PRODUCER.

From the success she has achieved, it's easy to assume that this has been her only career. On the contrary, working with million-dollar investment portfolios for high-net-worth individuals and corporations is Brenda's second career. Before Brenda started with the securities brokerage business in 1980, she spent ten stellar years in public relations at IBM. Her move from IBM to the investments world was well thought out, but Brenda says she is still questioned, on occasion, as to how she moved from one field to another. "People often say, 'How did you go from one particular industry to a different industry?'

I always answer, 'It's not so much the change as it is the desire.' I think being here is the closest I can be to having my own business and that was why I made the decision to change careers. I think you know when you go from one field to another if your skills will allow you to make an easy transition."

Though Brenda's various skills attributed greatly to her successful transition, the most important element was being a strong communicator. Brenda has a master's in communication from New York University. However, she contends that it doesn't take a master's in communications or an MBA, for that matter, to be good in her brokerage business. She explains, "I don't think people truly value the importance of being knowledgeable and effectively communicating that knowledge to others. In business that has great value." Brenda cites an experience of interviewing a young woman from Oklahoma City, her hometown, as an example of how important it is to be knowledgeable, particularly when starting out. "She was a young lady who was well versed on what goes on in the brokerage business. From my discussion with her, it was evident this lady had really done her homework. And the managers were really impressed by her, too. That is really a large part of doing well, I believe."

While it takes being both knowledgeable and a strong communicator, Brenda continues to explain that she enjoys working with people and that is probably the largest component of her success in the financial services business. "There's no way I could have reached this point if I didn't like listening to people talk. I think you have to be the type of person who likes being around people and feel comfortable in both professional and social settings. If not, how will people ever get to know you?" Brenda belongs to various professional organizations such as the National Association of Securities Professionals (NASP), an organization that seeks to enhance minority participation in the securities industry. But this seasoned Wall Street professional is not all business. Outside of the office she enjoys baseball and a good match on the tennis court. "My backhand is not what it used to be, but I still love the game," she says with a laugh. In addition to sports, Brenda is a very active member of her community. She is a member of three highly prominent community service organizations: The Links Inc., Alpha Kappa Alpha Sorority, and President of American Red Cross—Manhattan offices. Her involvement with these organizations allows her to give back in many ways. But the most gratifying feeling from her commitments comes from the young people she assists. She says, "Regardless of how successful one becomes, we all have a role to play. And that is to reach one and teach one."

Doing It for Herself

Almost every entrepreneur can recall a special experience or set of events that catapulted them into starting their own company. For Jacquette Timmons it was realizing that she could take the tools and strategies she mastered while working as an investment adviser in the private investment planning group, a division of the Private Bank at Bankers Trust Company and build her own investment management firm. When Bankers Trust decided in 1995 to close the private investment planning group for which Jacquette Timmons worked for four years, she asked herself that one critical question: "What's stopping me from doing this for myself?" The answer was a resounding—*nothing!* And with that thought she departed from Bankers Trust and did it for herself. In late 1995 Jacquette, using her own capital, launched Sterling Investment Management, Inc., a registered investment advisory firm. The company provides institutional investment management consulting services for small to midsize companies, nonprofit organizations, foundations, intermediary firms, and high-net-worth individuals with investable assets between $150 thousand and $100 million.

In speaking with Jacquette, thirty, an intensely focused businesswoman who has taken on the role of entrepreneur, it's apparent that she's quite happy with the new hat she wears as president and chief executive officer of Sterling Investment Management, Inc. Knowing when the time was right to venture out on her own came after overcoming her fear of uncertainty, the unknown. "Like most people who work for an organization, are on a career track, have an advanced degree, and are very good at what they do, I thought I was in a secure environment. The decision by Bankers Trust to dissolve my business was initially unsettling. But once I embraced uncertainty and realized that it is a part of living my life, I understood that I couldn't be so committed to the past and what was comfortable that I missed my opportunity for the future of my design.

"I could have taken one of three roads; first, I could have moved to another area of the company; second, I could have left and found another job; and third, I could have taken what I learned and created my own opportunity. There was never a doubt in my mind that the last choice would have been most fulfilling to me. But I also knew it was going to be very challenging." Jacquette's field is extremely competitive and has become more so with the entrance of companies that traditionally were not in the investment management industry, or for which investment management wasn't its main focus.

However, Jacquette explained that what makes

Sterling Investment Management, Inc., unique is that it is bringing to its client profile an institutional approach to the management of their assets—an approach that was previously available exclusively to Fortune 500 corporations or investors with assets greater than $100 million.

While the newly formed company has a niche, finding clients has been a challenge. Jacquette acknowledges that the company's "starting gate" problem can be linked to the firm's youth. The firm is nine months old and isn't a household name like a Bankers Trust or Merrill Lynch. However, as she has done in the past, Jacquette is turning this hurdle into an advantage for herself and her business.

Jacquette began her career on Wall Street ten years ago. Her first assignment at Bankers Trust Company was in human resources; she then worked for two years in operations and technology before moving into investment management. Jacquette obtained her MBA, in finance, from Fordham University's Graduate School of Business while working full-time at Bankers Trust Company; her undergraduate degree in marketing from the Fashion Institute of Technology. Although she has ten years of experience in the financial industry, some have perceived Jacquette's nontraditional route to investment management as a hurdle. She is often asked, how did someone with a background in fashion, human resources, and operation/technology end up as an investment adviser? She enthusiastically and confidently answers, "Although finance and fashion are different industries and human resources, operations and the role of investment manager require different technical skills, you still have to apply the same marketing principles to move your product or service from the seller to the buyer, and you adjust your delivery to correspond to the unique traits inherent in your respective industry."

Jacquette views this question in the same way as when she is asked about Sterling being able to compete against the Bankers Trusts and Merrill Lynches of the investment management world. When faced with such a question she responds, "By positioning my firm such that it can offer the resources of a major organization, access to the expertise of many firms, and the individual attention to detail of a boutique."

What people are also asking Jacquette, a frequent public speaker about entrepreneurship, is how she handles the biggest challenge of them all: "Doing it for herself as a single black woman?" The spiritually focused Western New York-raised woman answers, "For me, it begins with knowing that in order to enjoy life's journey, I need to be centered. I dedicate some time each day for introspection—asking for guidance, the ability to recognize my blessings, and the strength to learn from the challenges I face. My motto is to work and play hard—you have to have fun! I minimize my stress by working out every day, not getting upset when things don't go as I planned or envisioned, and trusting in my own individuality—a trait I picked up from my mother, a jazz singer who has always danced to her own drum.

"My last thought about being in business and 'doing it for myself?' Well, I'd say while you do it for yourself, you never do it alone—God is the driving force in my life. And through Him people have been brought into my life that have helped me in innumerable ways."

Glossary of Terms

U.S. Capital Markets: the financial markets where equity and debt are traded and where corporations and state and local governments can raise funds to finance their growth or invest in project(s). Since government entities are not private but public, they cannot raise capital through the equity markets.

Salesperson or Account Executive: the employee of a brokerage firm or investment bank who advises and handles orders for clients and has legal powers of an agent. Every account executive must pass certain tests and be registered with the NATIONAL ASSOCIATION OF SECURITIES DEALERS (NASD) before soliciting orders from customers. Also called registered representative.

Investment Banker: a firm acting as the underwriter or agent that serves as an intermediary between an issuer of securities and the investing public. In addition to their investment banking functions, the majority of investment bankers also maintain a broker-dealer operation, serving both wholesale and retail clients in brokerage and advisory capacities and offering a growing number of financially related services.

Corporate Bond or Debt: debt instrument issued by a private corporation. Corporate bonds typically have four distinguishing features: (1) they are taxable; (2) the have a par value of 1,000; (3) they have a term maturity—which means they come due all at once—and are paid out of a sinking fund accumulated for that purpose; (4) they are traded on major exchanges, with prices published in the newspaper.

Securities or Sales Accounts: relationship between a broker-dealer firm and its client wherein the firm, through its registered representative, acts as agent in buying and selling securities and sees to related administrative matters.

Organizations

National Black MBA Association
180 North Michigan, Suite 1820
Chicago, IL 60601

Black Women in Publishing
P.O. Box 6275
FDR Station
New York, New York 10150

National Association of Black Journalists
P.O. Box 17212
Washington, D.C. 20041

Sponsors for Educational Opportunity (SEO)
23 Gramercy Park South
New York, New York 10003

National Academy of Television Arts and Science
111 W. 57th St.
New York, New York 10019

InRoads Inc.
120 Wall Street
New York, New York 10005

The Girls' Vacation Fund, Inc.
370 Lexington Avenue
New York, New York 10017

References on Interviews

Baskerville, Donna M., Sheryl Hilliard Tucker, and Donna Whittingham-Barnes. "21 Women of Power and Influence in Corporate America." *Black Enterprise,* August 1991.

Bragg, Rick. "All she has, $150,000, is going to a university." *The New York Times*, August 13, 1995.

Downes, John, and Jordan E. Goodman. *Dictionary of Finance and Investment Terms.* New York: Barrons's, 1991.

Fisher, Anne. B. *Wall Street Women: Women in Power on Wall Street Today.* New York: Alfred A. Knopf, 1990.

Gaiter, Dorothy. "The Gender Divide: Black Women's Gains in Corporate America Outstrip Black Men's." *Wall Street Journal,* March 8, 1994.

Sellers, Valita. "As Black Women Rise in Professional Ranks: For Lack of Black Male Peers They Often Go

It Alone; A Bad Omen for Families?" *Wall Street Journal*, January 1986.

Steele, Carolyn Odom. "African-American Women Network Their Way to the Top." *Executive Female*, May/June 1995.

Tucker, Sheryl Hilliard. "Black Women in Corporate America: The Inside Story." *Black Enterprise*, August 1994.

Williams, Lena. "Not Just a White Man's Game: Blacks in Business Master the Art of Networking." *The New York Times*, November 9, 1995.

Woody, Bette. *Black Women in the Work Place: Impact of Structural Change in the Economy*. Connecticut: Greenwood Press, 1992.

KAREN GIBBS

Liberman, David. "CNN Venture Puts Spin on Business News." *USA Today*, December 28, 1995.

Tanouye, Elyse. "Women Traders Making Headway in the Futures Markets." *Wall Street Journal*, September 3, 1991.

BENITA PIERCE

Roberts, Sam. "Moving on Up: The Greening of America's Black Middle Class." *The New York Times*, June 8, 1995.

TERI AGINS

Bird, Laura and Teri Agins. "Bruised Barneys Seeks Shelter From Creditor." *The Wall Street Journal*, January 12, 1996.

Strom, Stephanie and Jennifer Steinhauer. "Haughty Couture Barneys; Barneys May Be Bankrupt, But its Founding Family Is Unbowed." *The New York Times*, January 21, 1996.

TONI BANKS

Edwards, Audrey and Craig K. Polite *Children of the Dream: Pyschology of Black Success*. New York: Anchor Books, 1992.

SANDRA STEVENS

Hayes, Cassandra. *Black Enterprise*. Entertainment/Industry Profiles, December 1995.

CAROL GREEN

Chance, Julia. "Form and Function." *Essence* magazine, April 1996.

LISA COWAN

Cole, Johnetta. *Straight Talk with America's Sister President*. New York: Anchor Books, 1994.

Tuck, Angela Duerson. "Spelman's camaraderie touches talks show host." *Atlanta Constitution*, May 17, 1993.

TERESA CLARKE

McCorduck, Pamela. "Scenarios for the 21st Century," *Wired*, April 1996.

GRACE VANDECRUZE

Lewis, Diane E. "Diversity and growth: Black MBA group has come far since its 70's beginning." *The Boston Globe*, September 29, 1995.

LISA CAESAR

Dean, Bob. "Don't count out gutsy, enterpising Hong Kong." *The Atlanta Journal Constitution*, June 30, 1996.

BITHIAH CARTER

King, Sharon."B.E. Investment Bank Overview: The Tough Get Going." *Black Enterprise*, June 1995.

Scott, Matthew S., Rhonda Reynolds, and Cassandra Hayes. "25 Years of Blacks in Financing." *Black Enterprise*, June 1993.